CW00727784

MATHS
PUZZLES
AND
GAMES

for ages 7-9

Contents

Introduction

Maths, Puzzles and Games 7-9 contains a wide range of puzzles and games that promote mathematical skills and logical thinking. Most of the activities are easy to administer and each of them forms a valuable element of a maths lesson. Each puzzle or game sheet features brief teacher's notes, which include a suggested objective.

The puzzles provide practice in a range of mental arithmetic skills and knowledge, such as revising addition, subtraction, multiplication and division facts, doubling, halving, adding two-digit numbers mentally, etc. Some children will solve some of the puzzles quite quickly, whilst others may take longer and may need extra support. In each case, encourage the children to follow logical steps to solve the puzzle. Once they can follow the patterns and relationships featured in a particular type of puzzle, give them further puzzles of this type to consolidate their understanding.

Games such as dominoes and bingo can help children gain some fundamental skills in an atmosphere of fun informality. Many children in the 7-9 age range still struggle with place value, so,

for example, the hundreds bingo, thousands bingo and decimals bingo games can provide a focus for discussion as well as repeated exposure to the place value patterns.

Some children are unfamiliar with the rules of traditional games such as dominoes. The dominoes games included in this book not only provide the chance for the children to learn how to play but also the opportunity to strengthen their mental arithmetic work.

THE CD-ROM
All of the activities are included on the accompanying CD-ROM to enable you to display them on the whiteboard for discussion purposes. You might prefer to print the sheets directly from the CD-ROM rather than to photocopy them from the book. Answers to all the puzzles are also provided on the CD-ROM.

Further mental maths puzzles can be found in our titles *Maths, Puzzles and Games for ages 9-11, Maths Mindstretchers for ages 7-9* and *Maths Mindstretchers for ages 9-11.*

Guidelines for assessing mathematics

You could use these pages as individual record sheets by highlighting the statements when you feel that pupils are secure in the specific skills that these represent.

<u>Level 1</u>

Using and applying mathematics

Pupils use mathematics as an integral part of classroom activities. They represent their work with objects or pictures and discuss it. They recognise and use a simple pattern or relationship.

- Do the children use mathematics as an integral part of classroom activities, eg with support? Do the children engage with practical mathematical activities involving sorting, counting and measuring by direct comparison? (Ma1 Level 1) ❑

- Do the children represent their work with objects or pictures? Do the children discuss their work? Do the children respond to questions and ideas from peers and adults? Do the children refer to the materials they have used and talk about what they have done, patterns they have noticed, etc? (Ma1 Level 1) ❑

- Do the children draw simple conclusions from their work? Do the children describe the different ways they have sorted objects, what is the same about objects in a set, how sets differ? (Ma1 Level 1) ❑

Number

Pupils count, order, add and subtract numbers when solving problems involving up to 10 objects. They read and write the numbers involved.

- Do the children count up to 10 objects? Do they estimate and check a number? Do they read and write numbers to 10? Do they order numbers to 10? (Ma2 Level 1) ❑

- Are the children beginning to use the fraction one half? (Ma2 Level 1) ❑

- Do the children understand addition as finding the total of two or more sets of objects? Do they understand subtraction as 'taking away' objects from a set and finding how many are left? (Ma2 Level 1) ❑

- Do the children add and subtract numbers of objects to 10? Are the children beginning to know some addition facts? (Ma2 Level 1) ❑

- Do the children solve addition/subtraction problems involving up to 10 objects? Do they solve problems involving 1p or £1 coins? (Ma2 Level 1) ❑

- Do the children record their work with objects, pictures or diagrams? Are they beginning to use the symbols + and = to record additions? (Ma2 Level 1) ❑

Shape, space and measures

When working with 2-D and 3-D shapes, pupils use everyday language to describe properties and positions. They measure and order objects using direct comparison and order events.

- Do the children use everyday language to describe properties of 2-D and 3-D shapes? Do they sort shapes and say how they have selected them? Do they use properties such as large, small, triangles, roll, stack? Are they beginning to refer to some features of shapes such as side and corner? Are they beginning to name the shapes they use in the context of an activity? (Ma3 Level 1) ❑

Andrew Brodie: Maths Puzzles and Games 7–9 © A&C Black 2011

- Do the children use everyday language to describe positions of 2-D and 3-D shapes? Do they respond to and use positional language, eg 'behind', 'under', 'on top of', 'next to', 'in between'? Do they respond to and use directional language in talk about objects and movement, eg 'forwards', 'backwards', 'turn'? (Ma3 Level 1) ❏

- Do the children measure and order objects using direct comparison? Do they order everyday events and describe the sequence? Do they use the vocabulary of time including days of the week? Do they read the time on an analogue clock at the hour and begin to know the half hour? (Ma3 Level 1) ❏

Handling data
Pupils sort objects and classify them, demonstrating the criterion they have used.

- Do the children sort and classify objects? Do they sort using one criterion or sort into disjoint sets using two simple criteria such as thick/thin? Do they sort objects again using a different criterion? Do they sort into a given large scale Venn or Carroll diagram? Do they represent their work by using the objects they have sorted as a record or using objects/pictures to create simple block graphs? (Ma4 Level 1) ❏

- Do they demonstrate the criterion they have used? Do they respond to questions about how they have sorted objects and why each object belongs in a set? Do they talk about which set has most? Do they talk about how they have represented their work? (Ma4 Level 1) ❏

Level 2

Using and applying mathematics

Pupils select the mathematics they use in some classroom activities. They discuss their work using some mathematical language and are beginning to represent it using symbols and simple diagrams. They explain why an answer is correct.

- Do the children select the mathematics they use in some classroom activities, eg with support? Do they find a starting point, identifying key facts/relevant information? Do they use apparatus, diagrams, role-play, etc. to represent and clarify a problem? Do they move between different representations of a problem, eg a situation described in words, a diagram, etc. Do they adopt a suggested model or systematic approach? Do they make connections and apply their knowledge to similar situations? Do they use mathematical content from Levels 1 and 2 to solve problems and investigate? (Ma1 Level 2) ❏

- Do the children discuss their work using mathematical language, eg with support? Do they describe the strategies and methods they use in their work? Do they engage with others' explanations, compare, evaluate? Are they beginning to represent their work using symbols and simple diagrams, eg with support? Do they use pictures, diagrams and symbols to communicate their thinking, or demonstrate a solution or process? Are they beginning to appreciate the need to record and develop their own methods of recording? (Ma1 Level 2) ❏

- Can the children explain why an answer is correct, eg with support? Can they predict what comes next in a simple number, shape or spatial pattern or sequence and give reasons for their opinion? (Ma1 Level 2) ❏

Number

Pupils count sets of objects reliably, and use mental recall of addition and subtraction facts to 10. They begin to understand the place value of each digit in a number and use this to order numbers up to 100. They choose the appropriate operation when solving addition and subtraction problems. They use the knowledge that subtraction is the inverse of addition. They use mental calculation strategies to solve number problems involving money and measures. They recognise sequences of numbers, including odd and even numbers.

- Do the children count sets of objects reliably, eg group objects in tens, twos or fives to count them? Are they beginning to understand the place value of each digit, using this to order numbers up to 100? Do they recognise sequences of numbers, including odd and even numbers, eg continue a sequence that increases or decreases in regular steps, recognise numbers from counting in tens or twos? (Ma2 Level 2) ❏

- Are the children beginning to use halves and quarters, eg in a practical context? Can they work out halves of numbers up to 20 and are they beginning to recall these? Can they relate the concept of half of a small quantity to the concept of half of a shape, eg shade one half or one quarter of a given shape? (Ma2 Level 2) ❏

- Do the children use the knowledge that subtraction is the inverse of addition, eg are they beginning to understand subtraction as 'difference'? Can they make related number sentences involving addition and subtraction? Do they understand halving as a way of 'undoing' doubling and vice versa? (Ma2 Level 2) ❏

- Do the children use mental recall of addition facts to 10, eg use place value to derive $30 + 70 = 100$ from the known fact $3 + 7 = 10$? Do they use mental calculation strategies to solve number problems including those involving money and measures? (Ma2 Level 2) ❏

Andrew Brodie: Maths Puzzles and Games 7–9 © A&C Black 2011

- Do the children choose the appropriate operation when solving addition and subtraction problems? Do they use repeated addition to solve multiplication problems? Are they beginning to use repeated subtraction or sharing equally to solve division problems? Can they solve number problems nvolving money and measures? (Ma2 Level 2) ❏

- Do they record their work in writing, eg record their mental calculations as number sentences? (Ma2 Level 2) ❏

Shape, space and measures

Pupils use mathematical names for common 3-D and 2-D shapes and describe their properties, including numbers of sides and corners. They distinguish between straight and turning movements, understand angles as a measure of turn, and recognise right angles in turns. They begin to use everyday non-standard and standard units to measure length and mass.

- Do the children use mathematical names for common 3-D and 2-D shapes, eg square, triangle, hexagon, pentagon, octagon, cube, cylinder, sphere, cuboid, pyramid? Do they describe their properties, including numbers of sides and corners? Do they make and talk about shapes referring to features and properties using language such as edge, face, corner? Do they sort 2-D and 3-D shapes according to a single criterion? Can they visualise frequently used 2-D and 3-D shapes? Are they beginning to understand the difference between shapes with two dimension and those with three? Do they recognise the properties that are the same even when a shape is enlarged? (Ma3 Level 2) ❏

- Can the children describe the position of objects, eg by using ordinal numbers (first, second, third, …)? Do they recognise that a shape stays the same even when it is held up in different orientations? Can they distinguish between straight and turning movements, eg between left and right and between clockwise and anticlockwise? Do they recognise right angles in turns? (Ma3 Level 2) ❏

- Do the children understand angle as a measure of turn, making whole turns, half turns and quarter turns? Are they beginning to use everyday non-standard and standard units to measure length and mass? Do they understand that numbers can be used to describe continuous measures? Do they know which measuring tools to use? Are they beginning to use a wider range of measures, eg a right angle checker or a time line? (Ma3 Level 2) ❏

Handling data

Pupils sort objects and classify them using more than one criterion. When they have gathered information, pupils record results in simple lists, tables and block graphs, in order to communicate their findings.

- Do the children sort objects and classify them using more than one criterion, eg sort a set of shapes using two criteria such as triangle/not triangle and blue/not blue? Do they understand the vocabulary related to handling data, such as 'sort', 'group', 'set', 'list', 'table', 'most common', 'most popular'? Can they collect and sort data to test a simple hypothesis? Can they record results in simple lists, tables, pictograms and block graphs? (Ma4 Level 2) ❏

- Can the children communicate their findings, using the simple lists, tables, pictograms and block graphs they have recorded, eg by responding to questions about the data they have presented and posing similar questions for others to answer? (Ma4 Level 2) ❏

Level 3

Using and applying mathematics

Pupils try different approaches and find ways of overcoming difficulties that arise when they are solving problems. They are beginning to organise their work and check results. Pupils discuss their mathematical work and are beginning to explain their thinking. They use and interpret mathematical symbols and diagrams. Pupils show that they understand a general statement by finding particular examples that match it.

- Do the children select the mathematics they use in a wider range of classroom activities? For example: Do they use classroom discussions to break into a problem, recognising similarities to previous work? Do they put the problem into their own words? Do they use mathematical content from levels 2 and 3? Do they choose their own equipment appropriate to the task, including calculators? ❑

- Do they try different approaches and find ways of overcoming difficulties that arise when they are solving problems? For example: Do they check their work and make appropriate corrections? Are they beginning to look for patterns in results as they work and do they use these to find other possible outcomes? (Ma1 Level 3) ❑

- Are the children beginning to organise their work and check results? For example: Are they beginning to develop their own ways of recording? Do they develop an organised approach as they get into recording their work on a problem? ❑

- Do they discuss their mathematical work and begin to explain their thinking? Do they use appropriate mathematical vocabulary? Do they talk about their findings by referring to their written work? ❑

- Do they use and interpret mathematical symbols and diagrams? (Ma1 Level 3) ❑

- Do the children understand a general statement by finding particular examples that match it? For example: Can they make a generalisation, with the assistance of probing questions and prompts? ❑

- Do they review their work and reasoning? For example: Do they respond to 'What if?' questions? When they have solved a problem, can they pose a similar problem for a partner? (Ma1 Level 3) ❑

Number

Pupils show understanding of place value in numbers up to 1000 and use this to make approximations. They begin to use decimal notation and to recognise negative numbers, in contexts such as money and temperature. Pupils use mental recall of addition and subtraction facts to 20 in solving problems involving larger numbers. They add and subtract numbers with two digits mentally and numbers with three digits using written methods. They use mental recall of the 2, 3, 4, 5 and 10 multiplication tables and derive the associated division facts. They solve whole number problems involving multiplication or division, including those that give rise to remainders. They use simple fractions that are several parts of a whole and recognise when two simple fractions are equivalent.

- Do the children understand place value in numbers to 1000? For example: Do they represent/compare numbers using number lines, 100 squares, base 10 materials, etc? Do they recognise that some numbers can be represented as different arrays? Do they use understanding of place value to multiply/divide whole numbers by 10 (whole number answers)? ❑

- Can the children use place value to make approximations? Do they recognise negative numbers in contexts such as temperature? Do they recognise a wider range of sequences, eg recognise sequences of multiples of 2, 5 and 10? (Ma2 Level 3) ❑

- Do the children use simple fractions that are several parts of a whole and recognise when two simple fractions are equivalent? Do they understand and use unit fractions such as $\frac{1}{2}, \frac{1}{4}, \frac{1}{3}, \frac{1}{5}, \frac{1}{10}$ and find those fractions of shapes and sets of objects? Do they recognise and record fractions that are several parts of the whole, such as $\frac{3}{4}, \frac{2}{5}$? Do they recognise some fractions that are equivalent to $\frac{1}{2}$? ❑

Andrew Brodie: Maths Puzzles and Games 7–9 © A&C Black 2011

- Are they beginning to use decimal notation in contexts such as money? For example: Can they order decimals with one decimal place or two decimal places in the context of money? Do they know that £3.06 equals 306p? (Ma2 Level 3) ❏

- Can the children derive associated division facts from known multiplication facts? Do they use inverses to find missing whole numbers in problems such as 'I think of a number, double it and add 5. The answer is 35. What was my number?'? ❏

- Are the children beginning to understand the role of the equals sign? For example: Can they solve 'balancing' problems such as $7 \times 10 = 82 - \square$? (Ma2 Level 3) ❏

- Can the children add and subtract two-digit numbers mentally? Can they use mental recall of the 2, 3, 4, 5 and 10 multiplication tables? Are they beginning to know multiplication facts for the 6, 7, 8 and 9 multiplication tables? (Ma2 Level 3) ❏

- Can the children use mental recall of addition and subtraction facts to 20 in solving problems involving larger numbers? Do they solve whole number problems including those involving multiplication or division that may give rise to remainders? (Ma2 Level 3) ❏

- Can the children add and subtract three-digit numbers using a written method? Can they multiply and divide two-digit numbers by 2, 3, 4, 5 or 10 with whole number answers and remainders? (Ma2 Level 3) ❏

Shape, space and measures

Pupils classify 3-D and 2-D shapes in various ways using mathematical properties such as reflective symmetry for 2-D shapes. They use non-standard units, standard metric units of length, capacity and mass, and standard units of time, in a range of contexts.

- Can the children classify 3-D and 2-D shapes in various ways using mathematical properties such as reflective symmetry for 2-D shapes? Do they sort objects and shapes using more than one criterion? Are they beginning to understand the terms regular and irregular? Do they recognise right angles in shapes in different orientations? Do they recognise angles that are bigger or smaller than 90°? Are they beginning to use the terms acute and obtuse? Do they recognise right-angled and equilateral triangles? Can they demonstrate that a shape has reflectional symmetry by folding? Do they recognise when a shape does not have a line of symmetry? Can they recognise common 3-D shapes? Can they relate 3-D shapes to drawings and photographs of them? Are they beginning to recognise nets of familiar 3-D shapes? (Ma3 Level 3) ❏

- Do the children recognise shapes in different orientations? Can they reflect shapes, presented on a grid, in a vertical or horizontal mirror line? Are they beginning to reflect simple shapes in a mirror line presented at 45°? Can they describe position and movement using terms such as left/right, clockwise/anticlockwise, quarter turn/90°? (Ma3 Level 3) ❏

- Do the children use non-standard units and standard metric units of length, capacity and mass in a range of contexts? For example: Can they measure a length to the nearest $\frac{1}{2}$ cm? Can they read simple scales? ❏

- Do they use standard units of time? Can they read a 12-hour clock and calculate time durations that do not go over the hour? ❏

- Do they use a wider range of measures? For example: Are they beginning to understand area as a measure of surface and perimeter as a measure of length? Are they beginning to find areas of shapes by counting squares? Do they recognise angles as a measure of turn and know that one whole turn is 360 degrees? (Ma3 Level 3) ❏

Handling data

Pupils extract and interpret information presented in simple tables and lists. They construct bar charts and pictograms, where the symbol represents a group of units, to communicate information they have gathered, and the interpret information presented in these forms.

- Can the children gather information by deciding what data to collect to answer a question and making appropriate choices for recording information? Can they construct bar charts and pictograms, where the symbol represents a group of units? Do they decide how best to present data, eg whether a bar chart, a pictogram or a Venn diagram would show the information most clearly? Can they decide upon an appropriate scale for a graph? Do they use Venn and Carroll diagrams to record their sorting and classifying of information? (Ma4 Level 3)   ❑

- Can the children extract and interpret information presented in simple tables, lists, bar charts or pictograms? Can they use a key to interpret data? Can they read scales labelled in twos, fives and tens, including reading between labelled divisions? Can they compare data? Can they respond to questions of a more complex nature such as 'How many children took part in this survey altogether?'? Can they understand the idea of certain and impossible relating to probability in the context of data regarding everyday situations? (Ma4 Level 3)   ❑

Andrew Brodie: Maths Puzzles and Games 7–9 © A&C Black 2011

Name _is Sydney Davey_   Date _____

Can you add mentally to solve the cross-number puzzle?

Find the numbers to fill the gaps. The first one has been done for you.

	Clues across	Clues down
a	16 + 7	b 28 + 6
c	37 + 7	d 39 + 3
		e 24 + 8
f	18 + 9	g 67 + 4
h	16 + 10	

Now make up your own addition cross-number puzzle.

	Clues across	Clues down
a		b
c		d
		e
f		g
h		

Teacher's notes

Suggested objective: *Add mentally combinations of one-digit and two-digit numbers.*

The activity sheet provides practice of mental work with addition and has the advantage of being self-checking.

Can you add mentally to solve the cross-number puzzle?

Find the numbers to fill the gaps. The first one has been done for you.

	a	b		
	4	6		
c		d	e	
f	g		h	i
	j	k		
		l		

Clues across	Clues down
a 39 + 7	b 58 + 5
	c 65 + 8
d 23 + 9	e 19 + 6
f 29 + 5	g 39 + 8
h 49 + 9	i 79 + 2
j 68 + 7	k 48 + 6
l 39 + 10	

Now make up your own addition cross-number puzzle.

	a	b		
c		d	e	
f	g		h	i
	j	k		
		l		

Clues across	Clues down
a	b
	c
d	e
f	g
h	i
j	k
k	

Teacher's notes

Suggested objective: *Add mentally combinations of one-digit and two-digit numbers.*

The activity sheet provides practice of mental work with addition and has the advantage of being self-checking.

Andrew Brodie: Maths Puzzles and Games 7-9 © A&C Black 2011

Can you add mentally to solve the cross-number puzzle?

Find the numbers to fill the gaps. The first one has been done for you.

Clues across	Clues down
a 26 + 7	b 28 + 10
c 9 + 7	d 58 + 7
e 73 + 9	f 16 + 8
g 48 + 8	h 56 + 10
i 36 + 6	i 38 + 7
j 32 + 9	
k 62 + 7	l 87 + 5
	m 49 + 8
n 66 + 7	o 28 + 8
p 58 + 11	q 87 + 7
r 39 + 9	

Teacher's notes

Suggested objective: *Add mentally combinations of one-digit and two-digit numbers.*

The activity sheet provides practice of mental work with addition and has the advantage of being self-checking.

Name _____ Date _____

Can you subtract mentally to solve the cross-number puzzle?

Find the numbers to fill the gaps. The first one has been done for you.

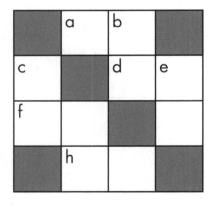

Clues across	Clues down
a 40 – 6	b 52 – 5
	c 36 – 8
d 81 – 3	e 92 – 7
f 92 – 6	g 71 – 8
h 48 – 9	

Now make up your own subtraction cross-number puzzle.

Clues across	Clues down
a	b
	c
d	e
f	g
h	

Teacher's notes

Suggested objective: *Subtract mentally combinations of one-digit and two-digit numbers.*

The activity sheet provides practice of mental work with subtraction and has the advantage of being self-checking.

Andrew Brodie: Maths Puzzles and Games 7–9 © A&C Black 2011

Name _____   *Date* _____

Can you subtract mentally to solve the cross-number puzzle?

Find the numbers to fill the gaps. The first one has been done for you.

	Clues across		Clues down
		a	51 – 4
b	34 – 8	c	70 – 7
d	82 – 9	e	41 – 7
f	46 – 8	g	91 – 6
h	51 – 9	i	30 – 9
j	24 – 7	k	82 – 8
l	54 – 5		

Now make up your own subtraction cross-number puzzle.

	Clues across		Clues down
		a	
b		c	
d		e	
f		g	
h		i	
j		k	
l			

Teacher's notes

Suggested objective: *Subtract mentally combinations of one-digit and two-digit numbers.*

The activity sheet provides practice of mental work with subtraction and has the advantage of being self-checking.

Name _____ Date _____

Can you subtract mentally to solve the cross-number puzzle?

Find the numbers to fill the gaps. The first one has been done for you.

a 3	b 4		c	d				
	e	f		g	h			
i		j	k		l	m		
n	o		p	q		r	s	
	t	u		v	w			
		x			y			

Clues across	Clues down
a 43 – 9	b 52 – 6
c 33 – 7	d 70 – 6
e 72 – 5	f 81 – 8
g 51 – 4	h 84 – 9
	i 23 – 5
j 44 – 6	k 92 – 7
l 62 – 8	m 54 – 9
n 90 – 8	o 28 – 5
p 59 – 7	q 33 – 7
r 61 – 5	s 70 – 1
t 37 – 6	u 24 – 8
v 70 – 9	w 21 – 6
x 71 – 9	
y 56 – 3	

Teacher's notes

Suggested objective: *Subtract mentally combinations of one-digit and two-digit numbers.*

The activity sheet provides practice of mental work with subtraction and has the advantage of being self-checking.

Andrew Brodie: Maths Puzzles and Games 7-9 © A&C Black 2011

Name _____ *Date* _____

Can you make triangles out of triangles?

1. Colour one small triangle.
2. Now colour four triangles together to make a bigger triangle.
3. Colour nine triangles to make a bigger triangle.
4. Colour sixteen triangles to make an even bigger triangle.

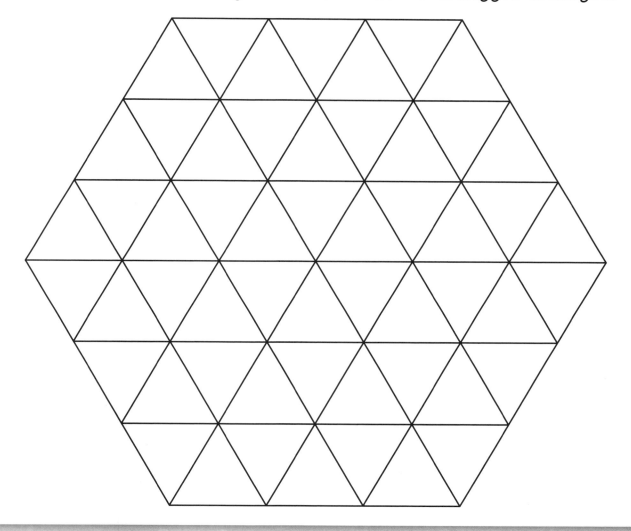

Teacher's notes

Suggested objective: *Describe, visualise, classify and draw shapes.*

Can the children visualise how to combine the small triangles to make triangles of different sizes? You could demonstrate with one or two examples on the whiteboard.

Name _____   Date _____

Can you make hexagons out of triangles?

Colour six small triangles to make a regular hexagon. How many different sized hexagons can you make by colouring the small triangles?

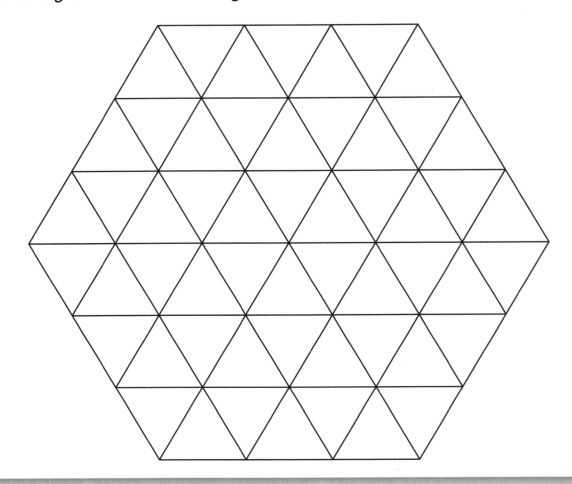

Teacher's notes

Suggested objective: *Describe, visualise, classify and draw shapes.*

Can the children visualise how to combine the small triangles to make hexagons of different sizes? You could demonstrate with one or two examples on the whiteboard.

Andrew Brodie: Maths Puzzles and Games 7–9 © A&C Black 2011

Name _____ **Date** _____

Can you make 10?

Join pairs of dots to make a total of 10. For example, join dot 1 on the vertical axis to dot 9 on the horizontal axis. Make sure you use a ruler!

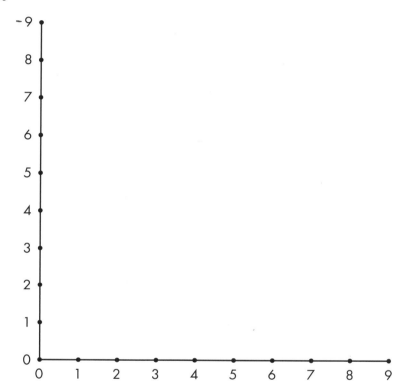

Here is one of the combinations you should have used:

1 + 9 = 10

Write down all the other combinations in the same way.

_____ _____ _____

_____ _____ _____

_____ _____

Teacher's notes

Suggested objective: *Derive and recall all addition and subtraction facts for each number to 20.*

The idea of creating curves from straight lines is of constant appeal to children. The combinations of numbers provide all the 'addition bonds' for 10.

Name _____   Date _____

Can you make 11?

Join pairs of dots to make a total of 11. For example, join dot 1 on the vertical axis to dot 10 on the horizontal axis. Make sure you use a ruler!

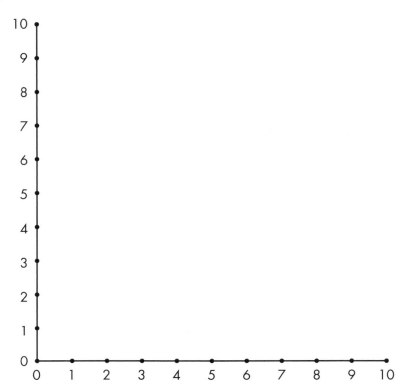

Here is one of the combinations you should have used:

1 + 10 = 11

Write down all the other combinations in the same way.

_____   _____   _____

_____   _____   _____

_____   _____   _____

Teacher's notes

Suggested objective: *Derive and recall all addition and subtraction facts for each number to 20.*

The combinations of numbers provide all the 'addition bonds' for 11.

Andrew Brodie: Maths Puzzles and Games 7–9 © A&C Black 2011

Name _____   Date _____

Can you make 12?

Join pairs of dots to make a total of 12. For example, join dot 1 on the vertical axis to dot 11 on the horizontal axis. Make sure you use a ruler!

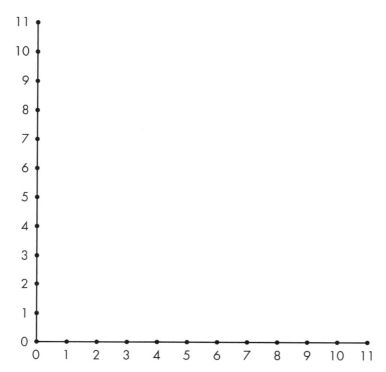

Here is one of the combinations you should have used:

1 + 11 = 12

Write down all the other combinations in the same way.

_____   _____   _____

_____   _____   _____

_____   _____   _____

_____

Teacher's notes

Suggested objective: *Derive and recall all addition and subtraction facts for each number to 20.*

The combinations of numbers provide all the 'addition bonds' for 12.

Name _____ Date _____

Can you make 13?

Join pairs of dots to make a total of 13. For example, join dot 1 on the vertical axis to dot 12 on the horizontal axis. Make sure you use a ruler!

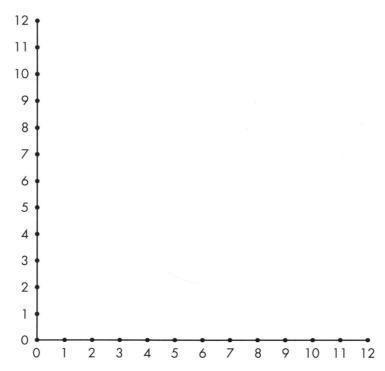

Here is one of the combinations you should have used:

1 + 12 = 13

Write down all the other combinations in the same way.

_____   _____   _____

_____   _____   _____

_____   _____   _____

_____   _____

Teacher's notes

Suggested objective: *Derive and recall all addition and subtraction facts for each number to 20.*

The combinations of numbers provide all the 'addition bonds' for 13.

Andrew Brodie: Maths Puzzles and Games 7–9 © A&C Black 2011

Name _____ Date _____

Can you make 14?

Join pairs of dots to make a total of 14. For example, join dot 1 on the vertical axis to dot 13 on the horizontal axis. Make sure you use a ruler!

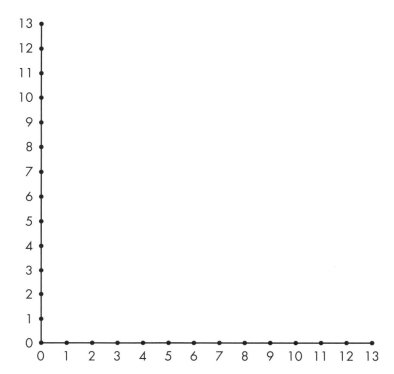

Here is one of the combinations you should have used:

1 + 13 = 14

Write down all the other combinations in the same way.

_____ _____ _____

_____ _____ _____

_____ _____ _____

_____ _____ _____

Teacher's notes

Suggested objective: *Derive and recall all addition and subtraction facts for each number to 20.*

The combinations of numbers provide all the 'addition bonds' for 14.

Name _____ Date _____

Can you make 15?

Join pairs of dots to make a total of 15. For example, join dot 1 on the vertical axis to dot 14 on the horizontal axis. Make sure you use a ruler!

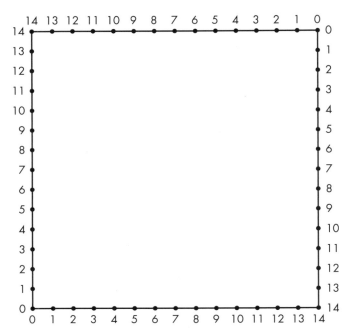

Here is one of the combinations you should have used:

1 + 14 = 15

Write down all the other combinations in the same way.

_____   _____   _____

_____   _____   _____

_____   _____   _____

_____   _____   _____

_____

Teacher's notes

Suggested objective: *Derive and recall all addition and subtraction facts for each number to 20.*

The combinations of numbers provide all the 'addition bonds' for 15. This time the grid is reflected to produce a double pattern.

Andrew Brodie: Maths Puzzles and Games 7-9 © A&C Black 2011

Name _____ Date _____

Can you make 16?

Join pairs of dots to make a total of 16. For example, join dot 1 on one axis to dot 15 on the other. Make sure you use a ruler!

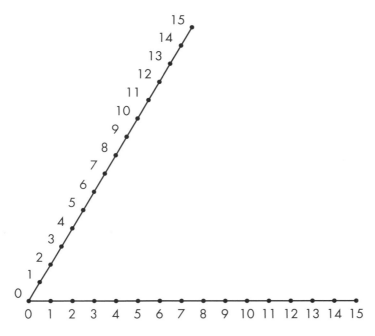

Here is one of the combinations you should have used:

1 + 15 = 16

Write down all the other combinations in the same way.

_____ _____ _____

_____ _____ _____

_____ _____ _____

_____ _____ _____

_____ _____

Teacher's notes

Suggested objective: *Derive and recall all addition and subtraction facts for each number to 20.*

The combinations of numbers provide all the 'addition bonds' for 16. This time the grid is reflected to produce a double pattern.

Name _____ Date _____

Can you make 17?

Join pairs of dots to make a total of 17. For example, join dot 1 on one axis to dot 16 on the other. Make sure you use a ruler!

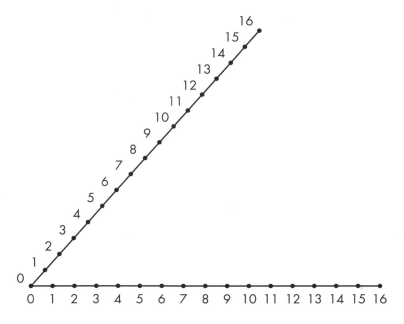

Here is one of the combinations you should have used:

1 + 16 = 17

Write down all the other combinations in the same way.

_____ _____ _____

_____ _____ _____

_____ _____ _____

_____ _____ _____

_____ _____ _____

Teacher's notes

Suggested objective: *Derive and recall all addition and subtraction facts for each number to 20.*

The combinations of numbers provide all the 'addition bonds' for 17. This time the grid is arranged at a different angle – ask the children to describe the effect of making the angle smaller than the previous ones used.

Andrew Brodie: Maths Puzzles and Games 7-9 © A&C Black 2011

Name _____ Date _____

Can you make 18?

Join pairs of dots to make a total of 18. For example, join dot 1 on one axis to dot 17 on the other. Make sure you use a ruler!

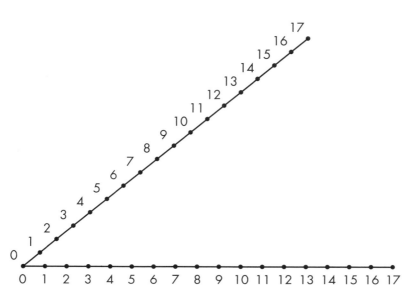

Here is one of the combinations you should have used:

1 + 17 = 18

Write down all the other combinations in the same way.

_____   _____   _____

_____   _____   _____

_____   _____   _____

_____   _____   _____

_____   _____   _____

_____

Teacher's notes

Suggested objective: *Derive and recall all addition and subtraction facts for each number to 20.*

The combinations of numbers provide all the 'addition bonds' for 18. This time the grid is arranged at a different angle – ask the children to describe the effect of making the angle smaller than the previous ones used.

Name _____ Date _____

Can you make 19?

Start by joining the dots on side C to the dots on side A. For example, join dot 1 on side C to dot 18 on side A, then join dot 2 to dot 17. Make sure you use a ruler!

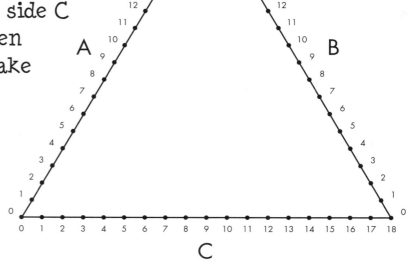

Write down all the other combinations. The first one has been done for you.

1 + 18 = 19

_____   _____   _____

_____   _____   _____

_____   _____   _____

_____   _____   _____

_____   _____   _____

Now you could join the dots on side B to the dots on side A, starting with joining dot 2 to dot 17.
Finally you could join matching numbers on side B to side C, starting with joining 1 to 1, then 2 to 2.

Teacher's notes

Suggested objective: *Derive and recall all addition and subtraction facts for each number to 20.*

The combinations of numbers provide all the 'addition bonds' for 19.

Andrew Brodie: Maths Puzzles and Games 7–9 © A&C Black 2011

Name _____ Date _____

Can you make 20?

Start by joining dot 0 on line A to dot 20 on line B, then join dot 1 to dot 19. Keep joining dots to make a total of 20. Make sure you use a ruler!

A

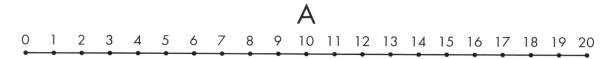

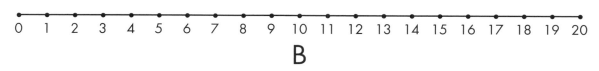

B

Write down all the other combinations in the same way. The first one has been done for you.

0 + 20 = 20

_____   _____   _____

_____   _____   _____

_____   _____   _____

_____   _____   _____

_____   _____   _____

_____   _____   _____

Teacher's notes

Suggested objective: *Derive and recall all addition and subtraction facts for each number to 20.*

The combinations of numbers provide all the 'addition bonds' for 20. How does the visual pattern differ to those on the previous sheets?

Name _____ *Date* _____

Can you make 20 and 22?

Start by joining the upper dots to the lower dots, finding every combination that adds up to 20. For example, join 0 to 20, then 1 to 19, 2 to 18 and so on. Now join the pairs that add up to 22: join 21 to 1, join 20 to 2, join 19 to 3 and so on.

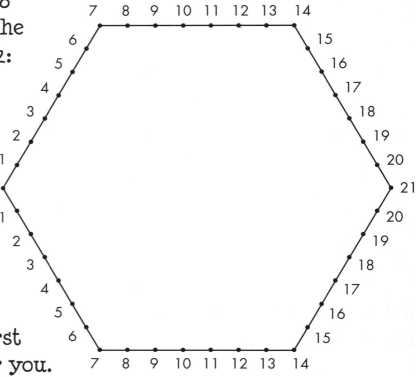

Write down all the combinations. The first one has been done for you.

1 + 21 = 22

_____   _____   _____

_____   _____   _____

_____   _____   _____

_____   _____   _____

_____   _____   _____

_____   _____   _____

_____   _____   _____

Teacher's notes

Suggested objective: *Derive and recall all addition and subtraction facts for each number to 20.*

This sheet goes beyond 20 as the pupils now have to find combinations of pairs of numbers to make 22. How can they describe the pattern that emerges in the centre of the diagram?

Andrew Brodie: Maths Puzzles and Games 7-9 © A&C Black 2011

Name _Sydney_   Date _6.10.1820_

How quickly can you complete each addition number train?

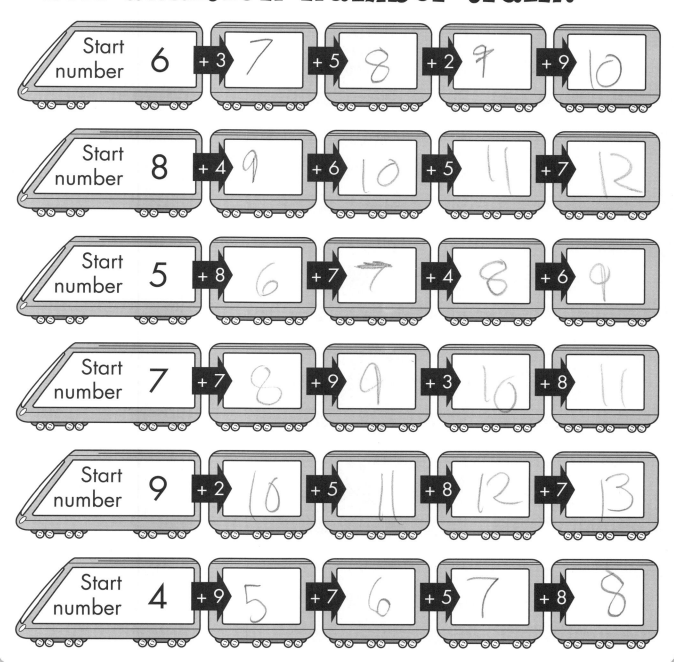

Start number 6 → +3 → 7 → +5 → 8 → +2 → 9 → +9 → 10

Start number 8 → +4 → 9 → +6 → 10 → +5 → 11 → +7 → 12

Start number 5 → +8 → 6 → +7 → 7 → +4 → 8 → +6 → 9

Start number 7 → +7 → 8 → +9 → 9 → +3 → 10 → +8 → 11

Start number 9 → +2 → 10 → +5 → 11 → +8 → 12 → +7 → 13

Start number 4 → +9 → 5 → +7 → 6 → +5 → 7 → +8 → 8

Teacher's notes

Suggested objective: *Derive and recall all addition facts for each number to 20.*

The children could use the class clock to time themselves completing each train.

Name _____ Date _____

How quickly can you complete each subtraction number train?

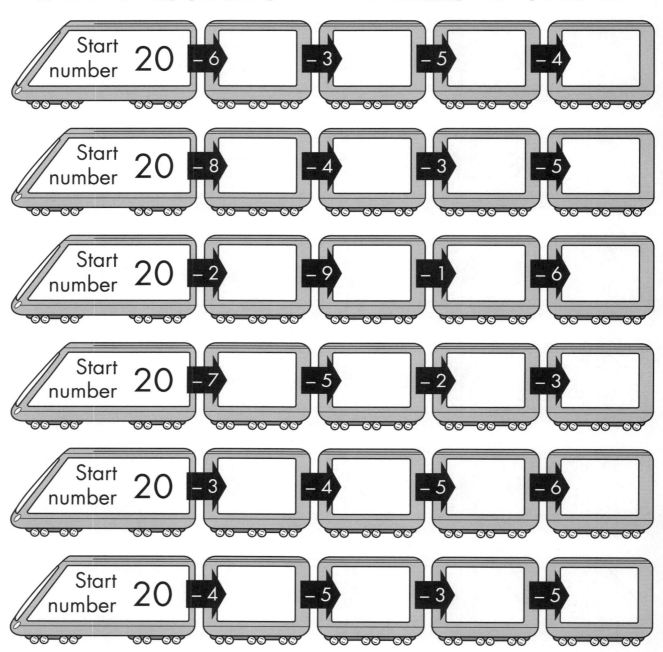

Start number 20 − 6 ▸ − 3 ▸ − 5 ▸ − 4 ▸

Start number 20 − 8 ▸ − 4 ▸ − 3 ▸ − 5 ▸

Start number 20 − 2 ▸ − 9 ▸ − 1 ▸ − 6 ▸

Start number 20 − 7 ▸ − 5 ▸ − 2 ▸ − 3 ▸

Start number 20 − 3 ▸ − 4 ▸ − 5 ▸ − 6 ▸

Start number 20 − 4 ▸ − 5 ▸ − 3 ▸ − 5 ▸

Teacher's notes

Suggested objective: *Derive and recall all subtraction facts for each number to 20.*

The children could use the class clock to time themselves completing each train.

Andrew Brodie: Maths Puzzles and Games 7–9 © A&C Black 2011

Name _____ **Date** _____

How quickly can you complete each number train?

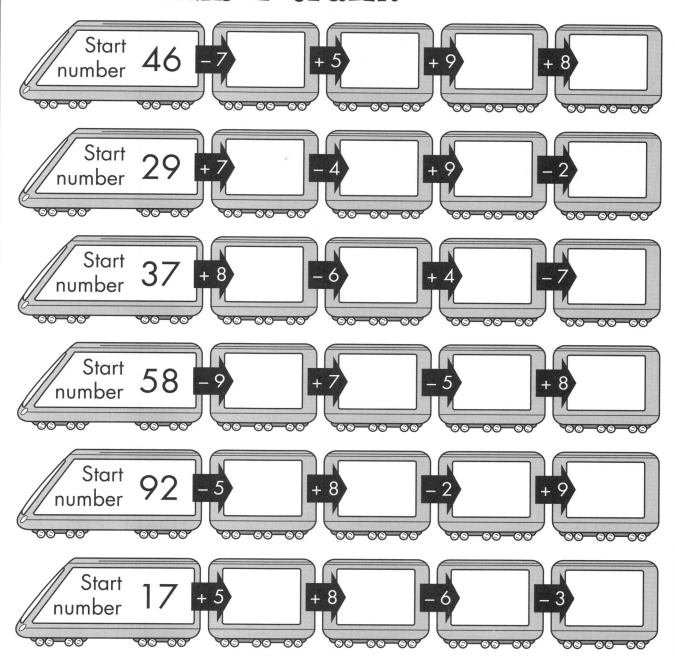

Start number **46** −7 ☐ +5 ☐ +9 ☐ +8 ☐

Start number **29** +7 ☐ −4 ☐ +9 ☐ −2 ☐

Start number **37** +8 ☐ −6 ☐ +4 ☐ −7 ☐

Start number **58** −9 ☐ +7 ☐ −5 ☐ +8 ☐

Start number **92** −5 ☐ +8 ☐ −2 ☐ +9 ☐

Start number **17** +5 ☐ +8 ☐ −6 ☐ −3 ☐

Teacher's notes

Suggested objective: *Add or subtract mentally combinations of one-digit and two-digit numbers.*

The children could use the class clock to time themselves completing each train.

Name _____ Date _____

Can you solve the arithmagons?

Look:

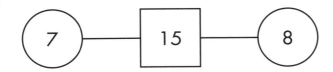

You can see that the number in the square is the sum of the numbers in the two circles.

In the same way, find the numbers that should be in the squares in this arithmagon.

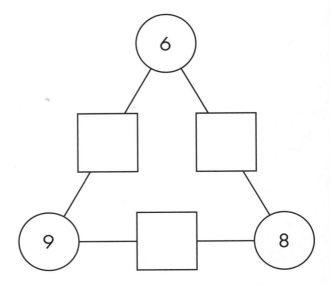

Now find the numbers that should go in the circles in this arithmagon.

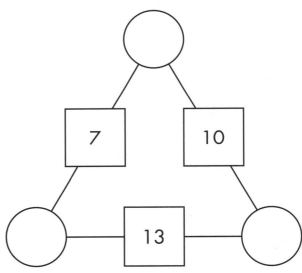

Teacher's notes

Suggested objective: *Solve one-step and two-step problems involving numbers.*

Ensure that the children understand how the arithmagon works: they must understand that the number in each square is the sum of the numbers in the adjacent circles. The second arithmagon is much more demanding than the first one and the children will need to use logic to determine the missing numbers.

Andrew Brodie: Maths Puzzles and Games 7–9 © A&C Black 2011

Name _____ Date _____

Can you solve the arithmagons?

Look:

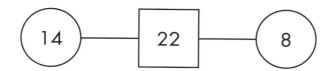

You can see that the number in the square is the sum of the numbers in the two circles.

In the same way, find the numbers that should be in the squares in this arithmagon.

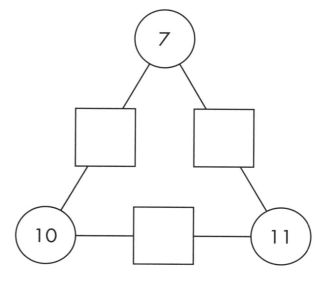

Now find the numbers that should go in the circles in this arithmagon.

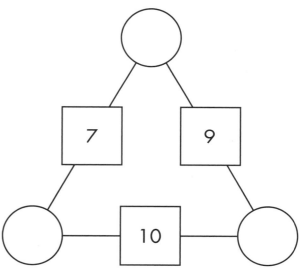

Teacher's notes

Suggested objective: *Solve one-step and two-step problems involving numbers.*

Ensure that the children understand how the arithmagon works: they must understand that the number in each square is the sum of the numbers in the adjacent circles. The second arithmagon is much more demanding than the first one and the children will need to use logic to determine the missing numbers.

Name _____ *Date* _____

Can you solve the arithmagons?

Look:

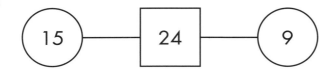

You can see that the number in the square is the sum of the numbers in the two circles.

In the same way, find the numbers that should be in the squares in this arithmagon.

Now find the numbers that should go in the circles in this arithmagon.

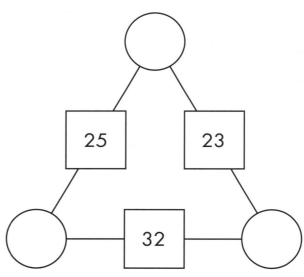

Teacher's notes

Suggested objective: *Solve one-step and two-step problems involving numbers.*

Ensure that the children understand how the arithmagon works: they must understand that the number in each square is the sum of the numbers in the adjacent circles. The second arithmagon is much more demanding than the first one and the children will need to use logic to determine the missing numbers.

Andrew Brodie: Maths Puzzles and Games 7–9 © A&C Black 2011

Name _____ **Date** _____

Can you solve the arithmagons?

Look:

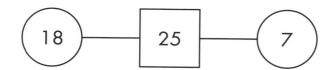

You can see that the number in the square is the sum of the numbers in the two circles.

In the same way, find the numbers that should be in the squares in this arithmagon.

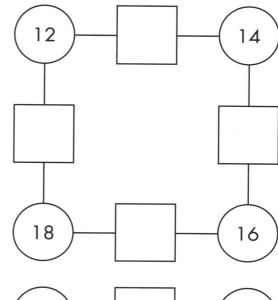

Now find the numbers that should go in the circles in this arithmagon.

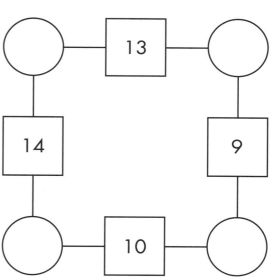

Teacher's notes

Suggested objective: *Solve one-step and two-step problems involving numbers.*

Ensure that the children understand how the arithmagon works: they must understand that the number in each square is the sum of the numbers in the adjacent circles. The second arithmagon is much more demanding than the first one and the children will need to use logic to determine the missing numbers.

Name _____ *Date* _____

Can you solve the arithmagons?

Look:

You can see that the number in the square is the sum of the numbers in the two circles.

In the same way, find the numbers that should be in the squares in this arithmagon.

Now find the numbers that should go in the circles in this arithmagon.

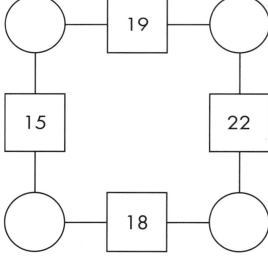

Teacher's notes

Suggested objective: *Solve one-step and two-step problems involving numbers.*

Ensure that the children understand how the arithmagon works: they must understand that the number in each square is the sum of the numbers in the adjacent circles. The second arithmagon is much more demanding than the first one and the children will need to use logic to determine the missing numbers.

Andrew Brodie: Maths Puzzles and Games 7–9 © A&C Black 2011

Name _____ Date _____

Can you solve the arithmagons?

Look:

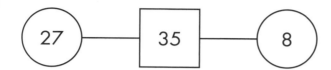

You can see that the number in the square is the sum of the numbers in the two circles.

In the same way, find the numbers that should be in the squares in this arithmagon.

Now find the numbers that should go in the circles in this arithmagon.

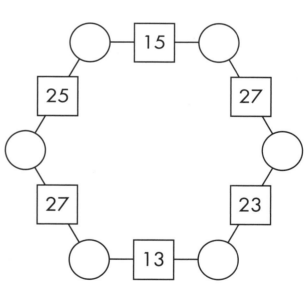

Teacher's notes

Suggested objective: *Solve one-step and two-step problems involving numbers.*

Ensure that the children understand how the arithmagon works: they must understand that the number in each square is the sum of the numbers in the adjacent circles. The second arithmagon is much more demanding than the first one and the children will need to use logic to determine the missing numbers.

Name _____ *Date* _____

Can you play hundreds bingo?

250		165		432
	144	297		256
487	547		965	

432	144		848	
412		776		747
		291	150	100

	250	165		848
412	382		654	
160			216	724

297	256		776	747
502	654	160		
		381		427

Teacher's notes

Suggested objective: *Recognise three-digit whole numbers.*

Th ese bingo cards should be used in conjunction with the number cards on sheet 31. Pupils should also be supplied with some blank cards or counters to cover their numbers as they are called out. 'Bingo' is called by a pupil when he/she makes one line.

Andrew Brodie: Maths Puzzles and Games 7–9 © A&C Black 2011

Name _____ **Date** _____

Can you play hundreds bingo?

250	165	432	144
297	256	487	547
965	848	412	776
747	291	150	100
382	654	160	216
724	502	381	427

Teacher's notes

Suggested objective: *Recognise three-digit whole numbers.*

These number cards should be used in conjunction with the bingo cards on sheet 30. The caller will call out each number at random for pupils to match to a number on their bingo card.

Name _____ **Date** _____

Can you play dominoes?

6 | 6	6 | 5	6 | 4
6 | 3	6 | 2	6 | 1
6 |	5 | 5	5 | 4
5 | 3	5 | 2	5 | 1
5 |		

Teacher's notes

Suggested objective: *Identify and match numbers quickly and accurately. Add, subtract, multiply and divide mentally.*

These domino cards can be used in conjunction with the dot domino cards and the calculation domino cards. Lower ability children can use them for number identification and for matching with the dot dominoes cards. Higher ability children will be able to use all three sets of dominoes interchangeably.

Andrew Brodie: Maths Puzzles and Games 7–9 © A&C Black 2011

Name _____ Date _____

Can you play dominoes?

4	4		4	6		4	2
4	1		4	0		3	3
3	2		3	1		3	
2	2		2	1		2	
1	1		1				

Teacher's notes

Suggested objective: *Identify and match numbers quickly and accurately. Add, subtract, multiply and divide mentally.*

These domino cards can be used in conjunction with the dot domino cards and the calculation domino cards. Lower ability children can use them for number identification and for matching with the dot dominoes cards. Higher ability children will be able to use all three sets of dominoes interchangeably.

Name _____ Date _____

Can you play dominoes?

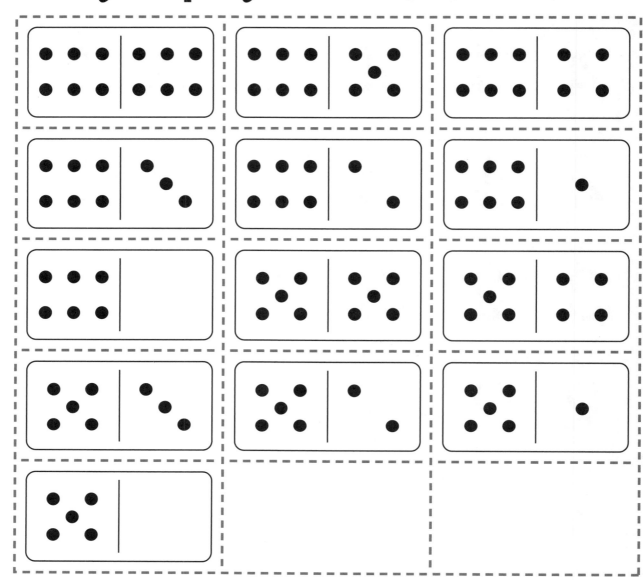

Teacher's notes

Suggested objective: *Identify and match numbers quickly and accurately. Add, subtract, multiply and divide mentally.*

These domino cards can be used in conjunction with the number domino cards and the calculation domino cards. Lower ability children can use them for number identification and for matching with the number dominoes cards. Higher ability children will be able to use all three sets of dominoes interchangeably.

Name _____   Date _____

Can you play dominoes?

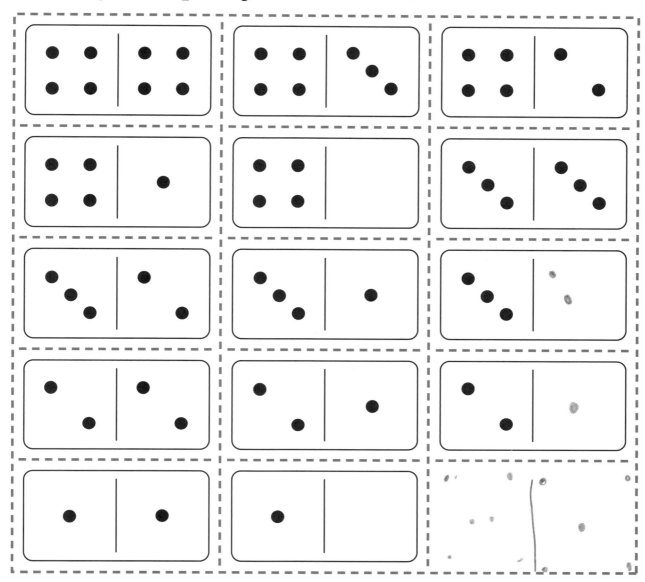

Teacher's notes

Suggested objective: *Identify and match numbers quickly and accurately. Add, subtract, multiply and divide mentally.*

These domino cards can be used in conjunction with the number domino cards and the calculation domino cards. Lower ability children can use them for number identification and for matching with the number dominoes cards. Higher ability children will be able to use all three sets of dominoes interchangeably.

Name _____ Date _____

Can you play dominoes?

| 12 ÷ 2 | 10 – 4 |

| 18 ÷ 3 | 11 – 6 |

| 13 × 2 | 16 ÷ 4 |

| 14 – 8 | 6 ÷ 2 |

| 2 × 3 | 11 – 9 |

| 24 ÷ 4 | 7 – 6 |

| 30 ÷ 5 | |

| 13 – 8 | 20 ÷ 4 |

| 12 – 7 | 20 ÷ 5 |

| 25 ÷ 5 | 11 – 8 |

| 15 ÷ 3 | 18 ÷ 9 |

| 11 – 6 | 9 – 8 |

| 20 ÷ 4 | |

Teacher's notes

Suggested objective: *Add, subtract, multiply and divide mentally.*

These domino cards can be used in conjunction with the number domino cards and the dot domino cards. Higher ability children will be able to use all three sets of dominoes interchangeably.

Andrew Brodie: Maths Puzzles and Games 7-9 © A&C Black 2011

Name _____ **Date** _____

Can you play dominoes?

| 2 × 2 | 12 ÷ 3 | 28 ÷ 7 | 12 – 9 | 13 – 2 | 16 ÷ 8 |

| 20 ÷ 5 | 15 – 14 | 36 ÷ 9 | | 21 ÷ 7 | 10 – 7 |

| 18 – 15 | 14 ÷ 7 | 24 ÷ 8 | 20 ÷ 19 | 27 ÷ 9 | |

| 18 ÷ 4 | 11 – 9 | 6 ÷ 3 | 7 – 6 | 18 ÷ 9 | |

| 1 × 1 | 3 ÷ 3 | 7 ÷ 7 | |

Teacher's notes

Suggested objective: *Add, subtract, multiply and divide mentally.*

These domino cards can be used in conjunction with the number domino cards and the dot domino cards. Higher ability children will be able to use all three sets of dominoes interchangeably.

Andrew Brodie: Maths Puzzles and Games 7–9 © A&C Black 2011

Name _____   Date _____

Can you write numbers in the circles to find the same totals?

Write the numbers 1, 2, 3, 4, 5 and 6 in the circles so that the joined numbers always add up to the same number.

What number is it? [ ]

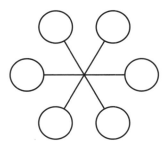

Write the numbers 8, 9, 10, 11, 12 and 13 in the circles so that the joined numbers always add up to the same number.

What number is it? [ ]

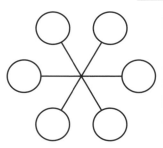

Write the numbers 5, 7, 9, 12, 14 and 16 in the circles so that the joined numbers always add up to the same number.

What number is it? [ ]

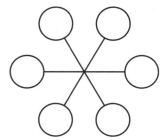

Write the numbers 8, 9, 12, 16, 19 and 20 in the circles so that the joined numbers always add up to the same number.

What number is it? [ ]

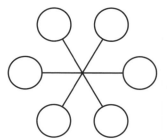

Teacher's notes

Suggested objective: *Identify patterns and relationships involving numbers.*

The children may be able to find the relationship between the numbers that enables them to find the common total.

Andrew Brodie: Maths Puzzles and Games 7–9 © A&C Black 2011

Name _____ Date _____

Can you write numbers in the circles to find the same totals?

Write the numbers 2, 3, 4, 5, 6 and 7 in the circles so that the joined numbers always add up to the same number.

What number is it? ☐

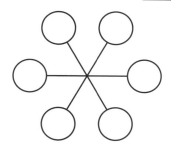

Write the numbers 45, 15, 25, 35, 20 and 40 in the circles so that the joined numbers always add up to the same number.

What number is it? ☐

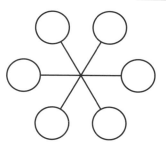

Write the numbers 8, 20, 4, 12, 24 and 16 in the circles so that the joined numbers always add up to the same number.

What number is it? ☐

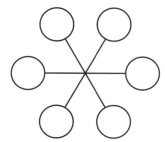

Write the numbers 27, 12, 32, 17, 37 and 22 in the circles so that the joined numbers always add up to the same number.

What number is it? ☐

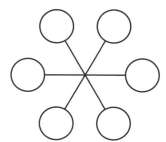

Teacher's notes

Suggested objective: *Identify patterns and relationships involving numbers.*

The children may be able to find the relationship between the numbers that enables them to find the common total.

Name _____   Date _____

Can you find the correct totals?

Write the numbers 1, 2, 3, 4, 5, 6, 7, 8 and 9 so that the three numbers in a line, including the one in the middle, always add up to 12.

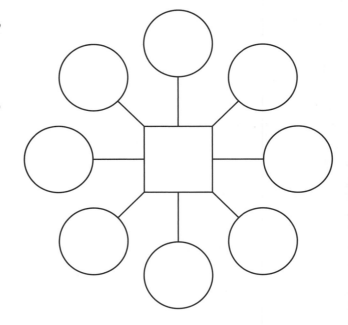

Write the numbers 2, 4, 6, 8, 10, 12, 14, 16 and 18 so that the three numbers in a line, including the one in the middle, always add up to 24.

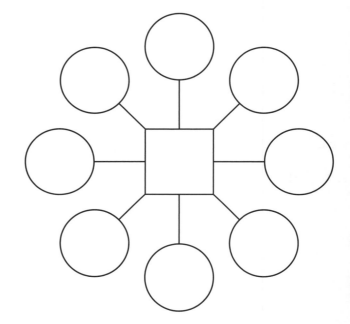

Teacher's notes

Suggested objective: *Identify patterns and relationships involving numbers.*

This puzzle is more demanding than those on sheets 38 and 39. The children may be able to find the relationship between the numbers that enables them to find the common total and they may find that their results for the first puzzle gives them clues to the second.

Andrew Brodie: Maths Puzzles and Games 7–9 © A&C Black 2011

Name _____   Date _____

Can you find the correct totals?

Write the numbers 5, 6, 7, 8, 9, 10, 11, 12 and 13 so that the three numbers in a line, including the one in the middle, always add up to 24.

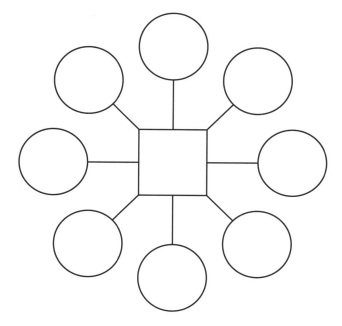

Write the numbers 4, 5, 6, 7, 8, 9, 10, 11 and 12 so that the three numbers in a line, including the one in the middle, always add up to 21.

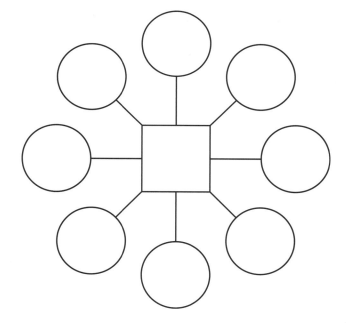

Teacher's notes

Identify patterns *and relationships involving numbers.*

This puzzle is more demanding than those on sheets 38 and 39. The children may be able to find the relationship between the numbers that enables them to find the common total and they may find that their results for the first puzzle gives them clues to the second.

Name _____ Date _____

Can you find the correct totals?

Write the numbers 5, 40, 25, 45, 10, 15, 35, 20 and 30 so that the three numbers in a line, including the one in the middle, always add up to the same total.

What is that total? ☐

Use the space below for working out the answer.

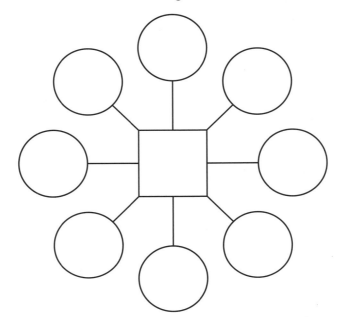

Teacher's notes

Suggested objective: *Identify patterns and relationships involving numbers.*

This puzzle is for more able pupils. The children may be able to find the relationship between the numbers that enables them to find the common total.

Andrew Brodie: Maths Puzzles and Games 7–9 © A&C Black 2011

Name _____ Date _____

Can you write numbers in the circles to find the same totals?

Write the numbers 1, 2, 3, 4, 5, 6, 7, 8, 9 and 10 in the circles so that the joined numbers always add up to the same number.

What number is it? [   ]

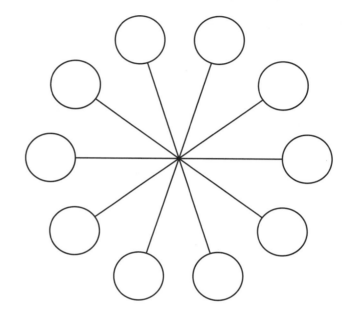

Write the numbers 2, 4, 6, 8, 10, 12, 14, 16, 18 and 20 in the circles so that the joined numbers always add up to the same number.

What number is it? [   ]

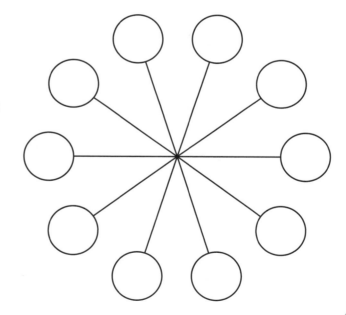

Teacher's notes

Suggested objective: *Identify patterns and relationships involving numbers.*

The children may be able to find the relationship between the numbers that enables them to find the common total.

Name _____   Date _____

Can you write numbers in the circles to find the same difference?

Write the numbers 2, 3, 4, 5, 6, 7, 8 and 9 in the circles so that the difference between the numbers on the end of each line is always equal to the 1 in the middle.

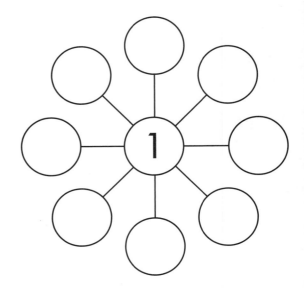

Write the numbers 18, 22, 20, 15, 18, 19, 17 and 21 in the circles so that the difference between the numbers on the end of each line is always equal to the 3 in the middle.

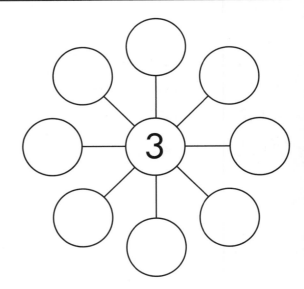

Teacher's notes

Suggested objective: *Identify patterns and relationships involving numbers.*

This activity sheet encourages the development of speed in subtraction but also serves as an introduction to the more difficult version of the activity to be found on sheet 45.

Andrew Brodie: Maths Puzzles and Games 7–9 © A&C Black 2011

Name _____ Date _____

Can you write numbers in the circles to find the same difference?

Write the numbers 4, 6, 12, 14, 17, 19, 25 and 27 in the circles so that the difference between the numbers on the end of each line is always equal to the same number in the middle.
What is that number? ☐

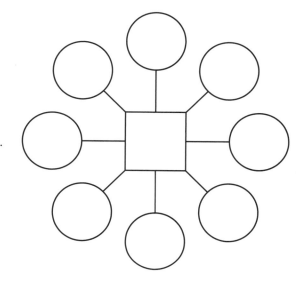

Write the numbers 9, 11, 12, 14, 15, 17, 18 and 20 in the circles so that the difference between the numbers on the end of each line is always equal to the same number in the middle.
What is that number? ☐

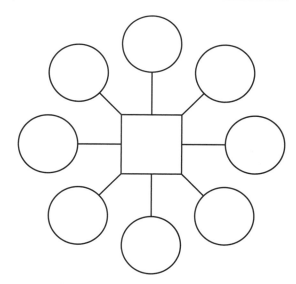

Teacher's notes

Suggested objective: *Identify patterns and relationships involving numbers.*

This activity sheet encourages the development of speed in subtraction.

Name _____ *Date* _____

Can you write the numbers in the correct places?

Use the numbers 1, 2, 3, 4, 5 and 6 to make a total of 11. You must use three numbers. You can use each number only once.

There are two pairs of numbers you can use to make a total of 11 if you start with the number 6. Look:

6 + 1 + 4 = 11   or   6 + 3 + 2 = 11

Find a way of making 11 if you start with the number 5.

5 + ☐ + ☐ = 11

Find ways of making 11 if you start with the number 4.

4 + ☐ + ☐ = 11   or   4 + ☐ + ☐ = 11

Write the numbers 1 to 6 in the small triangles to make each side of the large triangle add up to 11.

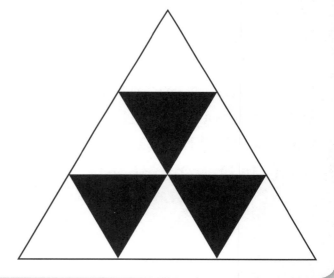

Teacher's notes

Suggested objective: *Derive and recall all addition and subtraction facts for each number up to 20.*

Ensure that the children understand the rule that each number can only be used once. Encourage them to use the results they have found when they attempt to solve the triangle puzzle.

Andrew Brodie: Maths Puzzles and Games 7–9 © A&C Black 2011

Name _____ Date _____

Can you write the numbers in the correct places?

Use the even numbers 2, 4, 6, 8, 10 and 12 to make a total of 18. You must use three numbers. You can use each number only once.

There is only one pair of numbers you can use to make a total of 18 if you start with the number 12. Look:

12 + 2 + 4 = 18

Find a way of making 18 if you start with the number 10.

10 + [   ] + [   ] = 18

Find a way of making 18 if you start with the number 8.

8 + [   ] + [   ] = 18

Write the numbers 2, 4, 6, 8, 10 and 12 in the small triangles to make each side of the large triangle add up to 18.

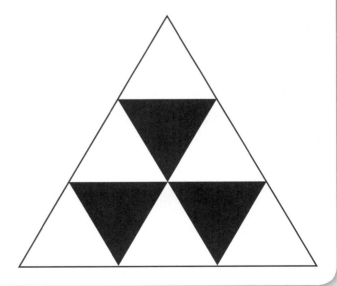

Teacher's notes

Derive and *recall all addition and subtraction facts for each number up to 20.*

Ensure that the children understand the rule that each number can only be used once. Encourage them to use the results they have found when they attempt to solve the triangle puzzle.

Name _____   *Date* _____

Can you write the numbers in the correct places?

Use the odd numbers 1, 3, 5, 7, 9 and 11 to make a total of 15. You must use three numbers. You can use each number only once.

There is only one pair of numbers you can use to make a total of 15 if you start with the number 11. Look:

11 + 1 + 3 = 15

Find a way of making 15 if you start with the number 9.

9 + ☐ + ☐ = 15

Find a way of making 15 if you start with the number 7.

7 + ☐ + ☐ = 15

Write the numbers 1, 3, 5, 7, 9 and 11 in the small triangles to make each side of the large triangle add up to 15.

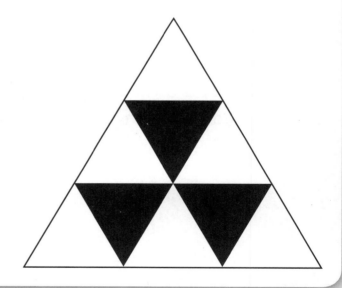

Teacher's notes

Suggested objective: *Derive and recall all addition and subtraction facts for each number up to 20.*

Ensure that the children understand the rule that each number can only be used once. Encourage them to use the results they have found when they attempt to solve the triangle puzzle.

Andrew Brodie: Maths Puzzles and Games 7–9 © A&C Black 2011

Name _____ Date _____

Can you write the numbers in the correct places?

Use the numbers 7, 8, 9, 10, 11 and 12 to make a total of 27. You must use three numbers. You can use each number only once.

There is only one pair of numbers you can use to make a total of 27 if you start with the number 12. Find a way of making 27 if you start with the number 12.

12 + [ ] + [ ] = 27

Find a way of making 27 if you start with the number 11.

11 + [ ] + [ ] = 27

Find a way of making 27 if you start with the number 10.

10 + [ ] + [ ] = 27

Write the numbers 7, 8, 9, 10, 11 and 12 in the small triangles to make each side of the large triangle add up to 27.

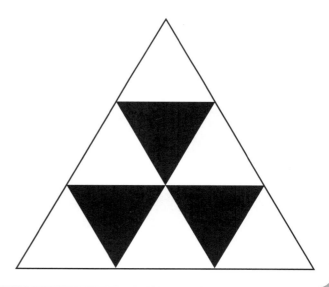

Teacher's notes

Add or *subtract mentally combinations of one-digit and two-digit numbers.*

Ensure that the children understand the rule that each number can only be used once. Encourage them to use the results they have found when they attempt to solve the triangle puzzle.

Name _____   Date _____

Can you write the numbers in the correct places?

Use the numbers 10, 11, 12, 13, 14 and 15 to make a total of 36. You must use three numbers. You can use each number only once.

There is only one pair of numbers you can use to make a total of 36 if you start with the number 15. Find a way of making 36 if you start with the number 15.

15 + ⬚ + ⬚ = 36

Find a way of making 36 if you start with the number 14.

14 + ⬚ + ⬚ = 36

Find a way of making 36 if you start with the number 13.

13 + ⬚ + ⬚ = 36

Write the numbers 10, 11, 12, 13, 14 and 15 in the small triangles to make each side of the large triangle add up to 36.

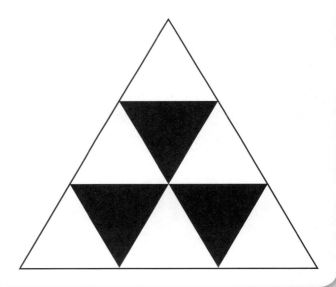

Teacher's notes

Suggested objective: *Add or subtract mentally combinations of one-digit and two-digit numbers.*

Ensure that the children understand the rule that each number can only be used once. Encourage them to use the results they have found when they attempt to solve the triangle puzzle.

Andrew Brodie: Maths Puzzles and Games 7-9 © A&C Black 2011

Name _____ Date _____

Can you write the numbers in the correct places?

Use the numbers 1, 2, 3, 4, 5, 6, 7 and 8 to make a total of 14. You must use three numbers. You can use each number only once.

There are two pairs of numbers you can use to make a total of 14 if you start with the number 8. Look:

8 + 5 + 1 = 14   or   8 + 4 + 2 = 14

Find ways of making 14 if you start with the number 7.

7 + ☐ + ☐ = 14   or   7 + ☐ + ☐ = 14   or   7 + ☐ + ☐ = 14

Find ways of making 14 if you start with the number 6.

6 + ☐ + ☐ = 14   or   6 + ☐ + ☐ = 14

Find ways of making 14 if you start with the number 5.

5 + ☐ + ☐ = 14   or   5 + ☐ + ☐ = 14   or   5 + ☐ + ☐ = 14

Find ways of making 14 if you start with the number 4.

4 + ☐ + ☐ = 14   or   4 + ☐ + ☐ = 14

Write the numbers 1 to 8 in the small squares to make each side of the large square add up to 14.

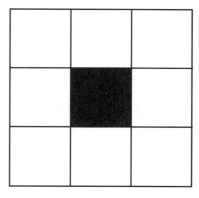

Teacher's notes

Suggested objective: *Derive and recall all addition and subtraction facts for each number up to 20.*

Ensure that the children understand the rule that each number can only be used once. Encourage them to use the results they have found when they attempt to solve the square puzzle.

Name _____ Date _____

Can you follow the directions on the grid?

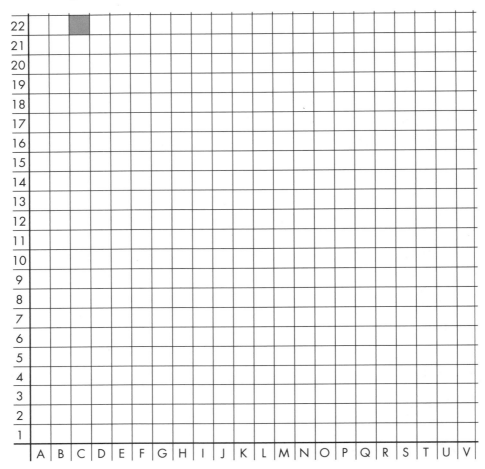

The square C22 has been shaded. Colour the following squares:
C21, C2o, C19, C18, F22, F2o, F19, F18, G22, G2o, G18, H22, H21,
H2o, H18, K22, K18, L22, L2o, L18, M22, M21, M2o, M19, M18,
P22, P21, P2o, P19, Q19, R2o, R19, R18, S19

Now choose some squares to colour and find the addresses (or coordinates) of your chosen squares.

Teacher's notes

Suggested objective: *Describe and identify the positions of squares on a grid of squares.*

The children could write their name or initials and give directions to others to find them on their own grids.

Andrew Brodie: Maths Puzzles and Games 7-9 © A&C Black 2011

Name _____ *Date* _____

Can you multiply mentally to solve the cross-number puzzle?

Find the numbers to fill the gaps. The first one has been done for you.

a 1		b	c
d 2	e		
	f	g	
		h	

Clues across	Clues down
	a 3 × 4
b 8 × 4	c 3 × 8
d 7 × 3	e 2 × 7
f 6 × 7	g 7 × 4
h 9 × 9	

Now make up your own multiplication cross-number puzzle.

a		b	c
d	e		
	f	g	
		h	

Clues across	Clues down

Teacher's notes

Suggested objective: *Multiply mentally using knowledge of multiplication facts.*

The activity sheet provides practice of mental work with multiplication and has the advantage of being self-checking.

Name _____ Date _____

Can you multiply mentally to solve the cross-number puzzle?

Find the numbers to fill the gaps. The first one has been done for you.

Clues across	Clues down
a 9 × 3	b 8 × 9
c 7 × 5	d 9 × 6
e 3 × 7	f 6 × 3
g 9 × 9	h 4 × 4
i 8 × 4	j 3 × 8
k 8 × 8	l 7 × 7
m 7 × 6	

Now make up your own multiplication cross-number puzzle.

Clues across	Clues down

Teacher's notes

Suggested objective: *Multiply mentally using knowledge of multiplication facts.*

The activity sheet provides practice of mental work with multiplication and has the advantage of being self-checking.

Andrew Brodie: Maths Puzzles and Games 7–9 © A&C Black 2011

Name _____ **Date** _____

Can you multiply mentally to solve the cross-number puzzle?

Find the numbers to fill the gaps. The first one has been done for you.

Grid	Clues

(Grid puzzle with cells labelled a–y; cell **a** = 3, cell **b** = 6)

Clues across	Clues down
a 6×6	b 7×9
c 2×7	d 5×9
e 8×4	f 5×5
g 8×7	h 7×9
	i 2×6
j 7×8	k 8×8
l 8×4	m 3×7
n 4×6	o 6×7
p 7×6	q 7×4
r 4×3	s 3×9
t 7×3	u 9×2
v 9×9	w 5×3
x 10×8	
y 6×9	

Teacher's notes

Suggested objective: *Multiply mentally using knowledge of multiplication facts.*

The activity sheet provides practice of mental work with multiplication and has the advantage of being self-checking.

Name _____ Date _____

Can you play addition bingo?

103		61		57
74	124		89	77
	78		115	

103	61		121	
	81	113		
63		70	69	43

57	74	121		81
	98		83	
100		94		27

124	89		113	
63		98	83	
	82	102		79

Teacher's notes

Suggested objective: *Subtract mentally pairs of two-digit numbers.*

These bingo cards should be used in conjunction with the calculation cards on sheet 57. Pupils should also be supplied with some blank cards or counters to cover their numbers as they are called out. 'Bingo' is called by a pupil when he/she completes a line.

Andrew Brodie: Maths Puzzles and Games 7–9 © A&C Black 2011

Name _____ Date _____

Can you play addition bingo?

64 + 39	27 + 34	18 + 39
46 + 28	89 + 35	72 + 17
19 + 58	63 + 15	79 + 36
97 + 24	48 + 33	62 + 51
26 + 37	44 + 26	52 + 17
19 + 24	35 + 63	36 + 47
75 + 25	78 + 16	12 + 15
37 + 45	64 + 38	42 + 37

Teacher's notes

Suggested objective: *Add mentally pairs of two-digit numbers.*

These addition cards should be used in conjunction with the bingo cards on sheet 56. The caller will call out each number at random for pupils to match to a number on their bingo card.

Name _____ **Date** _____

Can you play subtraction bingo?

		59		45
73	36		48	52
	58	8	6	

59		45	6	
	48	65		25
18		45		42

73		36	6	48
	74		5	
37		55		27

48	52		65	
25			74	5
51		32		17

Teacher's notes

Suggested objective: *Subtract mentally pairs of two-digit numbers.*

These bingo cards should be used in conjunction with the calculation cards on sheet 59. Pupils should also be supplied with some blank cards or counters to cover their numbers as they are called out. 'Bingo' is called by a pupil when he/she completes a line.

Andrew Brodie: Maths Puzzles and Games 7–9 © A&C Black 2011

Name _____ *Date* _____

Can you play subtraction bingo?

72 – 13	68 – 23	89 – 16
64 – 28	92 – 44	76 – 24
95 – 37	26 – 18	14 – 8
21 – 15	75 – 27	82 – 17
93 – 68	60 – 42	73 – 28
81 – 39	93 – 19	42 – 37
55 – 18	90 – 35	53 – 26
80 – 29	77 – 45	34 – 17

Teacher's notes

Suggested objective: *Subtract mentally pairs of two-digit numbers.*

These subtraction cards should be used in conjunction with the bingo cards on sheet 58. The caller will call out each number at random for pupils to match to a number on their bingo card.

Name _____ Date _____

Can you play multiplication bingo?

42			27		32
10			72	54	
28			12		56

42			27	30	
	12				81
16	36		48	45	

32			10	30	
12				24	63
		35	64	49	

72	54			81	
	16			24	
63	40	14			21

Teacher's notes

Suggested objective: *Recall multiplication facts.*

These bingo cards should be used in conjunction with the calculation cards on sheet 61. Pupils should also be supplied with some blank cards or counters to cover their numbers as they are called out.

Andrew Brodie: Maths Puzzles and Games 7–9 © A&C Black 2011

Name _____ Date _____

Can you play multiplication bingo?

6 × 7	3 × 9	4 × 8
5 × 2	8 × 9	9 × 6
7 × 4	2 × 6	8 × 7
6 × 5	4 × 3	9 × 9
2 × 8	4 × 9	6 × 8
5 × 9	3 × 8	9 × 7
5 × 7	8 × 8	7 × 7
5 × 8	2 × 7	3 × 7

Teacher's notes

Suggested objective: *Recall multiplication facts.*

These multiplication cards should be used in conjunction with the bingo cards on sheet 60. The caller will call out each number at random for pupils to match to a number on their bingo card.

Andrew Brodie: Maths Puzzles and Games 7–9 © A&C Black 2011

Name _____ Date _____

Can you find doubles to crack the code?

Code	
A	56
B	100
C	42
D	20
E	38
F	82
G	72
H	46
I	60
J	54
K	28
L	36
M	48
N	64
O	76
P	90
Q	68
R	88
S	32
T	30
U	24
V	26
W	34
X	44
Y	50
Z	52

15	38	10	28	25
30	76			

T O _ _ _

17	19

_ _

28	44	19

_ _ _

21	44	28	21	14	30	32	36

_ _ _ _ _ _ _ _

28

_

21	38	10	19

_ _ _ _

Teacher's notes

Suggested objective: *Identify the doubles of two-digit numbers.*

The children need to double each number provided in the word boxes to find a number to match with a letter. They write the letters found to create the words in a short sentence. The first word of the sentence is 'Today'.

Andrew Brodie: Maths Puzzles and Games 7-9 © A&C Black 2011

Name _____   **Date** _____

Code	
A	31
B	17
C	29
D	41
E	28
F	36
G	45
H	37
I	42
J	51
K	33
L	43
M	27
N	32
O	49
P	44
Q	39
R	18
S	23
T	26
U	14
V	47
W	24
X	38
Y	46
Z	48

Can you find halves to crack the code?

48	56
24	28

W E

62	36	56

— — —

28	46	84	64	90

— — — — —

74	62	86	94	56	46

— — — — — —

52	98

— —

72	84	64	82

— — — —

52	74	56

— — —

54	84	46	46	84	64	90

— — — — — — —

46	56	64	52	56	64	58	56

— — — — — — — —

Teacher's notes

Suggested objective: *Identify the halves of two-digit numbers.*

The children need to halve each number provided in the word boxes to find a number to match with a letter. They write the letters found to create the words in a short sentence. The first word of the sentence is 'We'.

Andrew Brodie: Maths Puzzles and Games 7-9 © A&C Black 2011

Name _____ Date _____

Can you solve the Sudoku?

Every box must have a □ ○ ⬡ ▭ △ ⬠

Every row must have a □ ○ ⬡ ▭ △ ⬠

Every column must have a □ ○ ⬡ ▭ △ ⬠

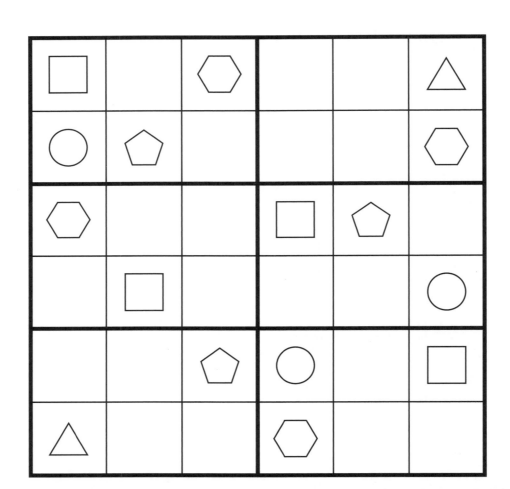

Teacher's notes

Suggested objective: *Solve one-step and two-step problems involving numbers.*

The children may find it easier to colour each of the shapes.

Andrew Brodie: Maths Puzzles and Games 7-9 © A&C Black 2011

Name _____ *Date* _____

Can you solve the Sudoku?

Every box must have a 1, 2, 3, 4, 5 and 6.

Every row must have a 1, 2, 3, 4, 5 and 6.

Every column must have a 1, 2, 3, 4, 5 and 6.

	3				
1		2	4	3	
4		3			1
	1		3		
3	6		2		5
	4				3

Teacher's notes

Suggested objective: *Solve one-step and two-step problems involving numbers.*

The children may find it easier to write lightly in pencil before committing to final answers.

Name _____ Date _____

Can you follow compass directions?

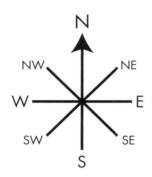

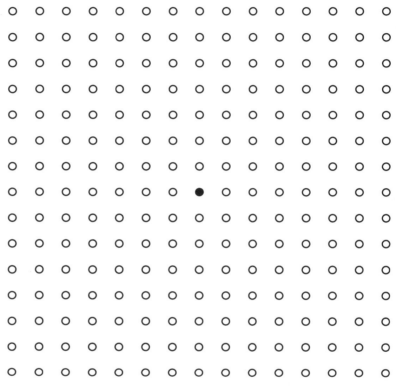

1. Start at the centre spot.
2. Move four spots to the North, then colour the spot.
3. Now move three points to the North-East and colour the spot.
4. Move three points to the South-East and colour the spot.
5. Move four spots to the South and colour the spot.
6. Move three spots to the South-West and colour the spot.
7. Draw straight lines to join the spots, then join the last spot to the first spot.

   What shape have you made? [_____]

Teacher's notes

Suggested objective: *Use the eight compass points to describe direction.*

Pupils could make up their own instructions for others to follow.

Andrew Brodie: Maths Puzzles and Games 7–9 © A&C Black 2011

Name _____ Date _____

Can you play squares?

Play with a partner.

1. Take it in turns to draw a line from one spot to another spot next to it. Move only in a horizontal or vertical line.

2. If you get a chance to make a complete square you should write your initial in it and you are allowed to draw an extra line.

3. Sometimes you may get a chance to complete lots of squares. Write your initial in every square you draw.

4. When no more squares can be drawn count the number of squares each person has claimed.

5. The winner is the person with most squares.

Teacher's notes

Suggested objective: *Devise strategies to work logically.*

The children should identify and use patterns, relationships and properties of shapes when competing to complete squares.

Name _____ Date _____

Can you play thousands bingo?

1346	2400		8619	7000
	5200	6278		
9814		7250		4025

	1346	2400		3800
	6950	4700	3694	
9284			8800	6000

8619		7000	3800	6950
	4650		8007	
9348		2750	5000	

5200		6278	4700	
	3694	4650		8007
9500		1842		2605

Teacher's notes

Suggested objective: *Recognise four-digit whole numbers.*

These bingo cards should be used in conjunction with the number cards on sheet 69. Pupils should also be supplied with some blank cards or counters to cover their numbers as they are called out.

Andrew Brodie: Maths Puzzles and Games 7–9 © A&C Black 2011

Name _____ Date _____

Can you play thousands bingo?

1346	2400	8619
7000	5200	6278
9814	7250	4025
3800	6950	4700
3694	9284	8800
6000	4650	8007
9348	2750	5000
9500	1842	2605

Teacher's notes

Suggested objective: *Recognise four-digit whole numbers.*

These number cards should be used in conjunction with the bingo cards on sheet 68. The caller will call out each number at random for pupils to match to a number on their bingo card.

Name _____ Date _____

Can you play decimals bingo?

1.5	2.3		3.7	4.6
	5.2		2.75	
3.25		4.12		9.86

1.5		2.3	0.5	
	0.75	6.4		8.2
	5.82		4.39	9.06

3.7		4.6		0.5
	0.75		9.42	3.02
	4.25	6.8	8.33	

5.2		2.75		6.4
	8.2	9.42	3.02	
7.45		4.02		0.9

Teacher's notes

Suggested objective: *Recognise decimal numbers.*

These bingo cards should be used in conjunction with the number cards on sheet 71. Pupils should also be supplied with some blank cards or counters to cover their numbers as they are called out.

Andrew Brodie: Maths Puzzles and Games 7–9 © A&C Black 2011

Name _____ Date _____

Can you play decimals bingo?

1.5	2.3	3.7
4.6	5.2	2.75
3.25	4.12	9.86
0.5	0.75	6.4
8.2	5.82	4.39
9.06	9.42	3.02
4.25	6.8	8.33
7.45	4.02	0.9

Teacher's notes

Suggested objective: *Recognise decimal numbers.*

These number cards should be used in conjunction with the bingo cards on sheet 70. The caller will call out each number at random for pupils to match to a number on their bingo card.

Andrew Brodie: Maths Puzzles and Games 7-9 © A&C Black 2011

Name _____ Date _____

Can you identify the correct numbers?

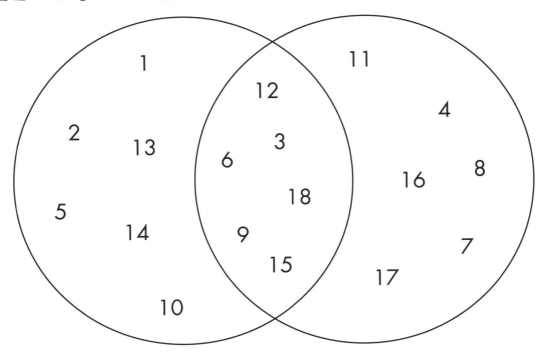

Which numbers are in the right circle but not the left?

Which numbers are in the left circle but not the right?

Which numbers are in both circles?

What is special about the numbers in both circles?

Teacher's notes

Suggested objective: *Analyse and interpret the data in a Venn diagram.*

This puzzle requires the pupils to interpret the wording of the questions correctly.

Andrew Brodie: Maths Puzzles and Games 7-9 © A&C Black 2011

Name _____ Date _____

Can you identify the correct numbers?

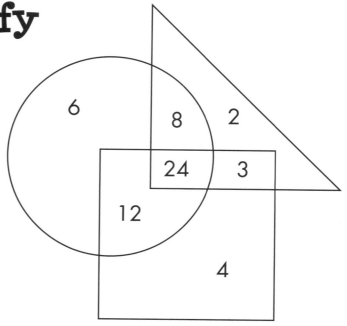

Which number is in the circle only? ☐

Which number is in the triangle only? ☐

Which number is in the square only? ☐

Which number is in the circle and square but not the triangle? ☐

Which number is in the circle and triangle but not the square? ☐

Which number is in the triangle and square but not the circle? ☐

Which number is in all three shapes? ☐

What is special about the number that is in all three shapes? ☐

Teacher's notes

Suggested objective: *Analyse and interpret the data in a shapes diagram.*

This puzzle requires the pupils to interpret the wording of the questions correctly.

Andrew Brodie: Maths Puzzles and Games 7–9 © A&C Black 2011

Name _____ Date _____

Can you find all the squares?

How many squares can you see in this picture? [   ]

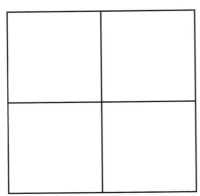

How many squares can you see in this picture? [   ]

Teacher's notes

Suggested objective: *Identify and use properties of shapes.*

You may wish to supply the pupils with sheet 76 so that they can experiment with finding the squares.

Andrew Brodie: Maths Puzzles and Games 7-9 © A&C Black 2011

Name _____ **Date** _____

Can you find all the rectangles?

How many rectangles can you see in this picture? [   ]

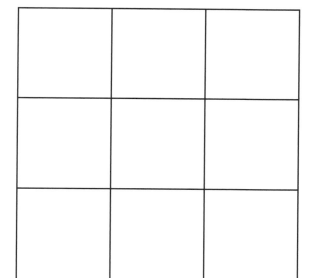

How many rectangles can you see in this picture? [   ]

Teacher's notes

Suggested objective: *Identify and use properties of rectangles.*

You may wish to supply the pupils with sheet 76 so that they can experiment with finding the rectangles.

Name _____   Date _____

Practice sheet for sheets 74 and 75

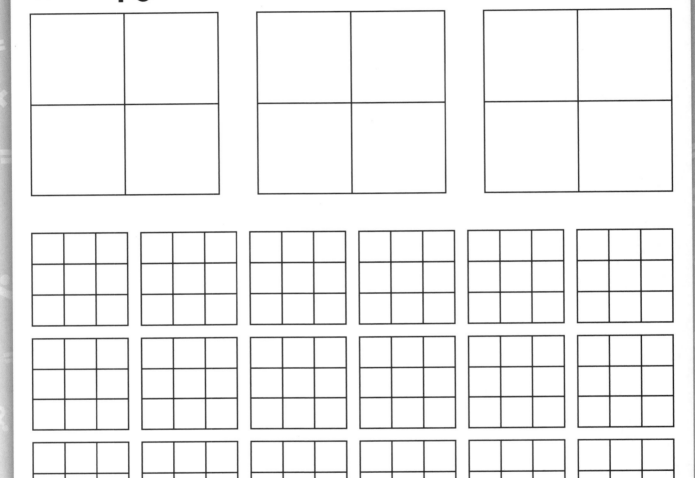

Teacher's notes

Suggested objective: *Identify and use properties of shapes.*

You may wish to supply the pupils with this practice sheet as they work on sheets 74 and 75.

Andrew Brodie: Maths Puzzles and Games 7–9 © A&C Black 2011

Name _____ Date _____

Can you find the odd one out in each set?

Circle the odd one out in each set below.

1.

2.

3.   3   8   12   9

4.

5.   25   40   65   31

6.   5   55   75   25

7.

8.   36   30   42   7

9.   16   18   81   45

Teacher's notes

Suggested objective: *Identify and use patterns, relationships and properties of numbers or shapes.*

The children may suggest more than one answer as the odd one out but should be encouraged to make the 'best choice'.

Name _____ *Date* _____

Can you follow the patterns?

Look at the diagram below.

If you follow a horizontal arrow (→)
you need to add 4.

If you follow a vertical arrow (↓)
you need to add 2.

Write the missing numbers in the boxes.

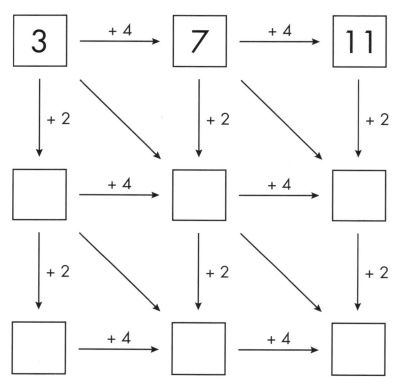

What addition could be written next to each diagonal (↘)
arrow? Insert it on the diagram.

Teacher's notes

Identify and *use patterns, relationships and properties of numbers.*

This activity will provide practice in addition as well as in logical thinking. Help the pupils to understand how the diagram works. Can they identify the relationship between the numbers that are arranged diagonally?

Andrew Brodie: Maths Puzzles and Games 7–9 © A&C Black 2011

Name _____ Date _____

Can you follow the patterns?

Look at the diagram below.

If you follow a horizontal arrow (→)
you need to add 6.

If you follow a vertical arrow (↓)
you need to subtract 2.

Write the missing numbers in the boxes.

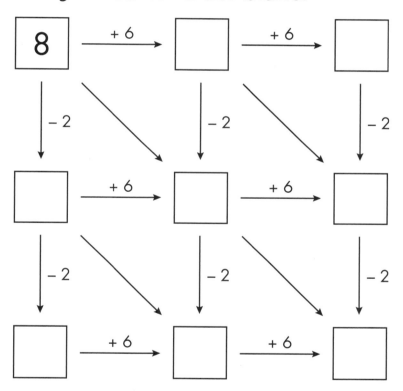

What addition could be written next to each diagonal (↘)
arrow? Insert it on the diagram.

Teacher's notes

Suggested objective: *Identify and use patterns, relationships and properties of numbers.*

This activity will provide practice in addition and subtraction as well as in logical thinking. Help the pupils
to understand how the diagram works. Can they identify the relationship between the numbers that are
arranged diagonally?

Name _____ Date _____

Can you find and follow the patterns?

Look at the diagram below.

For every horizontal arrow (→) you must always add the same number.

For every vertical arrow (↓) you must always add the same number.

Write the missing numbers in the boxes.

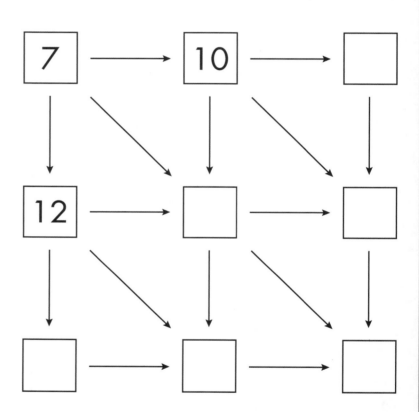

What addition could be written next to each arrow (→ ↓ ↘)?
Write them on the diagram.

Teacher's notes

Suggested objective: *Identify and use patterns, relationships and properties of numbers*

This activity will provide practice in addition and subtraction as well as in logical thinking. Help the pupils to understand how the diagram works. Can they identify the relationship that each arrow represents?

Andrew Brodie: Maths Puzzles and Games 7–9 © A&C Black 2011

Name _____   *Date* _____

Can you follow the patterns?

Look at the diagram below below.

If you follow a horizontal arrow (→)
you need to multiply by 3.

If you follow a vertical arrow (↓)
you need to multiply by 2.

Write the missing numbers in the boxes.

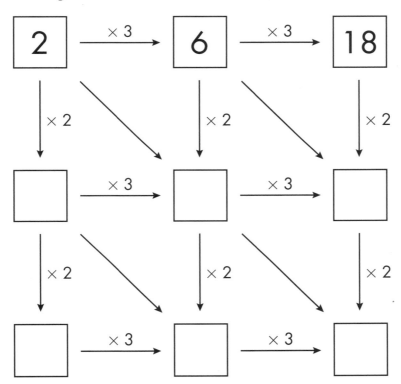

What multiplication could be written next to each diagonal
arrow (↘)? Write it in the diagram.

Teacher's notes

Suggested objective: *Identify and use patterns, relationships and properties of numbers.*

This activity will provide practice in multiplication as well as in logical thinking. Help the pupils to
understand how the diagram works. Can they identify the relationship between the numbers that are
arranged diagonally?

Andrew Brodie: Maths Puzzles and Games 7–9 © A&C Black 2011

Name _____ *Date* _____

Can you follow the patterns?

Look at the diagram below.

If you follow a horizontal arrow (→)
you need to multiply by 3.

If you follow a vertical arrow (↓)
you need to multiply by 4.

Write the missing numbers in the boxes.

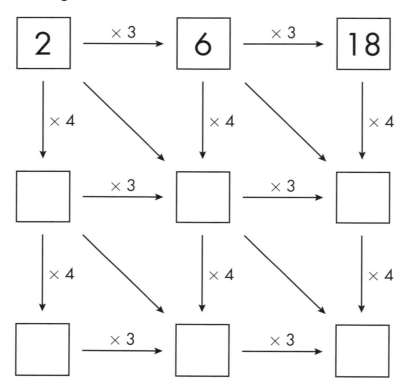

What multiplication could be written next to each diagonal
arrow (↘)? Write it in the diagram.

Teacher's notes

Suggested objective: *Identify and use patterns, relationships and properties of numbers.*

This activity will provide practice in multiplication as well as in logical thinking. Help the pupils to
understand how the diagram works. Can they identify the relationship between the numbers that are
arranged diagonally?

Andrew Brodie: Maths Puzzles and Games 7–9 © A&C Black 2011

Name _____ *Date* _____

Can you follow the patterns?

Look at the diagram below.

If you follow a horizontal arrow (→)
you need to multiply by 3.

If you follow a vertical arrow (↓)
you need to multiply by 2.

Write the missing numbers in the boxes.

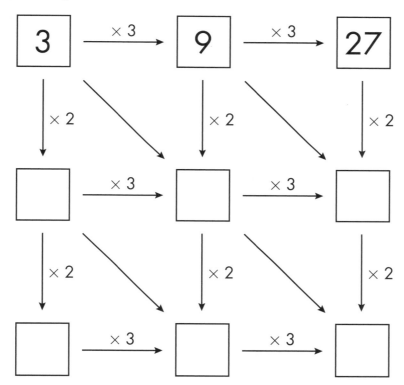

What multiplication could be written next to each diagonal
arrow (↘)? Write it in the diagram.

Teacher's notes

Identify and *use patterns, relationships and properties of numbers.*

This activity will provide practice in multiplication as well as in logical thinking. Help the pupils to understand how the diagram works. Can they identify the relationship between the numbers that are arranged diagonally?

Name _____ Date _____

Can you find and follow the patterns?

Look at the diagram below.

For every horizontal arrow (→) you must always multiply by the same number.

For every vertical arrow (↓) you must always multiply by the same number.

Write the missing numbers in the boxes.

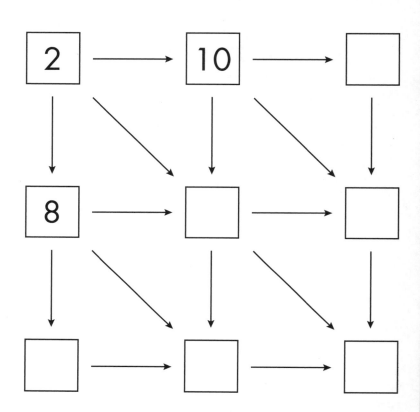

What multiplication could be written next to each arrow (→ ↓ ↘)? Write them on the diagram.

Teacher's notes

Suggested objective: *Identify and use patterns, relationships and properties of numbers.*

This activity will provide practice in multiplication and division as well as in logical thinking. Help the pupils to understand how the diagram works. Can they identify the relationship that each arrow represents?

Andrew Brodie: Maths Puzzles and Games 7–9 © A&C Black 2011

Name _____ *Date* _____

Can you find and follow the patterns?

Look at the diagram below.

For every horizontal arrow (→) you must always multiply by the same number.

For every vertical arrow (↓) you must always multiply by the same number.

Write the missing numbers in the boxes.

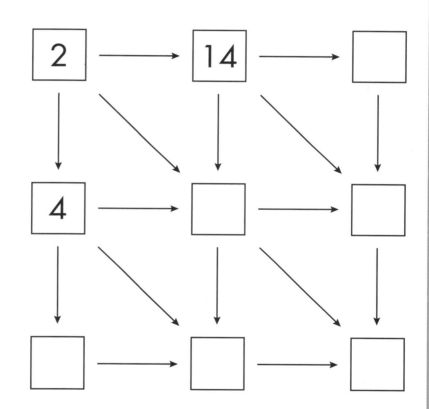

What multiplication could be written next to each arrow (→ ↓ ↘)? Write them on the diagram.

Teacher's notes

Suggested objective: *Identify and use patterns, relationships and properties of numbers.*

This activity will provide practice in multiplication and division as well as in logical thinking. Help the pupils to understand how the diagram works. Can they identify the relationship that each arrow represents?

Name _____ Date _____

Can you find and follow the patterns?

Look at the diagram below.

For every horizontal arrow (→) you must always divide by the same number.

For every vertical arrow (↓) you must always divide by the same number.

Write the missing numbers in the boxes.

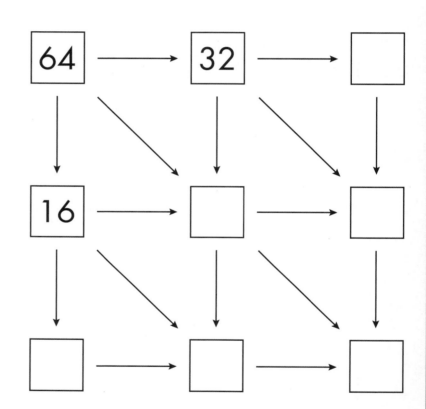

What multiplication could be written next to each arrow (→ ↓ ↘)? Write them on the diagram.

Teacher's notes

Suggested objective: *Identify and use patterns, relationships and properties of numbers.*

This activity will provide practice in multiplication and division as well as in logical thinking. This puzzle requires advanced skills in division. Can the pupils identify the relationship that each arrow represents?

Andrew Brodie: Maths Puzzles and Games 7-9 © A&C Black 2011